LABORATORY MANUAL TO ACCOMPANY

PUNTOS DE PARTIDA

AN INVITATION TO SPANISH

MARÍA SABLÓ-YATES

Delta College

Listening Passages contributed by
Ana María Pérez-Gironés
Wesleyan University

Note: This Laboratory Manual accompanies *Puntos de partida: An Invitation to Spanish,* Fourth Edition, by Knorre, Dorwick, Glass, and Villarreal.

EDITION 4

McGraw-Hill, Inc.

New York   St. Louis   San Francisco   Auckland   Bogotá   Caracas
Lisbon   London   Madrid   Mexico City   Milan   Montreal   New Delhi
San Juan   Singapore   Sydney   Tokyo   Toronto

This is an  book.

Laboratory Manual to accompany
Puntos de partida:
An Invitation to Spanish

3 4 5 6 7 8 9 0 MAL MAL 9 0 9 8 7 6 5 4

ISBN 0-07-035895-8

This book was typed in Palatino on a Macintosh by Chris de Heer/Desktop by Design.
The editors were Thalia Dorwick, Alice Mace Nakanishi, and Jane Parkinson.
The production supervisor was Diane Renda.
Production and editorial assistance was provided by Lorna Lo, Ann Potter, and Stacey Sawyer.
Illustrations were by David Bohn, Wayne Clark, Axelle Fortier, Lori Heckelman, Stephanie O'Shaughnessy, Barbara Reinertson, Katherine Tillotson, Stan Tusan, and Joe Veno.
The printer and binder was Malloy Lithographing, Inc.

Grateful acknowledgment is made for use of the following materials: *Page 27 Diario de Juarez,* Editora del Norte; *46* © Antonio Mingote; *86* © Quino; *108 left* Casa Glez; *108 right* Chopin; *109 left* Microstar; *109 right* Audio Bonpland; *123* Megacentro; *150* © Instituto Roit; *151* © Laboratorio Sais; *152* © Quino; *165* © Antonio Mingote; *197* © Antonio Mingote; *202 Semana; 203 Semana; 208* © Quino; *238* Riviera Paquetes; *242* Universidad de Cantabria; *244* © Quino.

Contents

To the Student

The purpose of the tape program that accompanies *Puntos de partida* is to give you as much practice as possible in listening to and speaking, reading, and writing, and, above all, understanding the Spanish language in a variety of contexts. This edition of the Laboratory Manual contains a variety of exercises to help you accomplish that goal. To get the most out of the tape program, you should listen to the tapes after your instructor covers the corresponding material in class, and you should listen as often as possible. You will need the Laboratory Manual much of the time when you listen to the tapes, since many of the exercises are based on visuals, realia (real things—such as advertisements, classified ads, and so on—that you would encounter in a Spanish-speaking country), and written cues.

The tape program follows the format of chapters in the main text. Each chapter begins with a section (**Vocabulario: Preparación**) in which you can practice vocabulary in a variety of contexts. This preliminary vocabulary study is followed by pronunciation exercises (**Pronunciación y ortografía**). The minidialogues from the text are followed by exercises and activities on the grammatical concepts of the chapters (**Minidiálogos y gramática**), and by functional dialogue practice (**Situaciones**). Each chapter ends with a section that combines grammar points and vocabulary introduced in the chapter (**Un poco de todo: Para entregar**). This final section is to be handed in to your instructor for correction; no answers are provided on the tape or in the Answers appendix at the back of the manual. In addition, some exercises give you the option of answering in writing (**Preguntas**, follow-ups to **Situaciones**). Since writing the answers to these exercises is an option only, you should ask your instructor how she or he would prefer these to be handled.

You will find additional review sections (**Repasos**) after Chapters 3, 6, 9, 12, and 18. Each **Repaso** contains a number of exercises labeled **Para entregar** that are to be handed in to your instructor. We have made an effort to reintroduce vocabulary and grammar from previous chapters in these review sections, and throughout the Laboratory Manual, so that you have the opportunity to use the grammatical structures and the vocabulary you have learned in a variety of contexts and situations.

The exercises and activities in most sections progress from controlled to more open-ended and personalized or interactive, to give you a chance to be more creative in Spanish while practicing the skills you have learned. With the exception of the **Para entregar** portions of the Laboratory Manual, the **Dictados,** and other writing-based activities, you will hear the answers to most exercises on the tape immediately after the item or at the end of a series of items. You will find the answers to most written exercises (except those called **Para entregar**) in the appendix.

Although the tape program includes some material taken directly from *Puntos de partida*, it also contains many new exercises: surveys (**Encuestas;** dictations; personalized questions and interviews; visually based listening comprehension exercises; new cultural listening passages, some based on survey questions answered by native speakers; activities based on realia; additional brief dialogues, some interactive in nature; and, beginning in Chapter 11, songs. Whenever possible, the exercises are presented in a context.

The following types of exercises are a regular feature of the *Puntos de partida* tape program and are found in most chapters.

- **Definiciones, Situaciones,** and **Asociaciones** use a multiple choice or matching format in order to test listening comprehension and vocabulary.

- **Identificaciones** and **Descripción,** as their names imply, will ask you to generate responses based on visuals, with or without written or oral cues. Although these are more controlled in nature, they are contextualized and related to the theme of the current or a previous chapter. You will find these types of exercises throughout the Laboratory Manual.

- **Encuestas** are personalized surveys in which you need only check an answer that is true for you. These surveys are offered for listening comprehension and are related to the theme of the chapter or to specific grammar points. You will find these at the beginning of both the vocabulary and the grammar sections.

- **Los hispanos hablan** is a new feature of the fourth edition on the Laboratory Manual. The section, found after **Vocabulario: Preparación,** presents comments from native speakers on a variety of topics: clothing, pastimes, favorite foods, and so on. Each section of **Los hispanos hablan** is tied to the theme and/or the vocabulary of the chapter in which it is found. The passages offer listening comprehension that is based on cultural information. The follow-up activities include taking notes, evaluating true or false statements, making comparisons, completing charts, and answering questions.

- The **Minidiálogos** are, with few exceptions, the same ones that appear in *Puntos de partida.* They offer examples of real-life situations and often convey cultural information. Although the text for the minidialogues does not appear in the Laboratory Manual (unless they are **Dictados**), the corresponding exercises generally do. The follow-up exercises include cloze dictations, true or false statements, summarizing statements, identifying the person who made a statement, and inferring information from the dialogue. The minidialogues appear at the beginning of each grammar section.

- There are two types of questions and answer sequences: **Preguntas** and **Entrevista.** The **Preguntas** will offer you an oral or written cue, and you will hear the correct answer on the tape after each item. **Entrevista** activities, in contrast, offer no cues or answers. The questions are more open-ended and personalized, and you will be able to stop the tape to write your answers. The **Preguntas** are usually found at the end of a grammar section. The **Entrevista** is a regular feature of the **Un poco de todo** section that is for handing in to your instructor.

- The **Situaciones** dialogues are taken from the textbook. Like the minidialogues, they offer examples of real-life conversations and situations, as well as some cultural information. After they are read on tape, you will usually have the opportunity to participate in a similar conversation, interactive in nature, in which you use the cues that are provided. In some instances, you may have the option of writing your answers. You will always hear a correct answer on the tape.

- Listening passages appear in the **Un poco de todo** section. These passages are cultural in nature and contain information on a variety of topics related to the Hispanic world. Their themes are related to the theme of each chapter. The passages are usually preceded by a section called **Antes de escuchar** in which you will practice listening strategies guessing content, gisting, making inferences about the passage, and so on. Following each passage is a **Después de escuchar** section that offers a variety of comprehension or follow-up exercises.

- The Laboratory Manual also includes many types of dictations (**Dictados**) and other writing activities. You will be asked to listen for and write down specific information: letters, words, phrases, or entire sentences. In some instances, you will be asked to jot down notes about the content of brief passages. Answers are generally provided in the appendix.

Sound effects are used throughout the tape program, when appropriate. You will hear a variety of native speakers, so that you can get used to different accents and voice types found in the Spanish-speaking world, but no accent will be so pronounced as to be difficult for you to understand. In approximately the first third of the tape program, the speakers will speak at a slower rate. The rate of speech will increase gradually until it reaches natural or close to natural speed in the final third of the tape program.

Learning another language requires hard work and patience, as well as an open mind. We hope that the variety of exercises and the cultural information in the Laboratory Manual will provide a natural and stimulating context within which you will begin to communicate in Spanish!

We offer our sincere thanks to the following individuals: to Ana María Pérez-Gironés (Wesleyan University), who wrote the listening passages in **Un poco de todo**; to the Hispanic exchange students whose answers were the bases of the passages in the **Los hispanos hablan;** to Marc Accornero, whose voice is heard on the songs and who was instrumental in their selection; to William R. Glass

(Pennsylvania State University), whose reading of the previous edition of the manual provided welcome suggestions and advice; to Thalia Dorwick, whose comments, suggestions, and superior editing made this Laboratory Manual and tape program possible; and to my family for their support and understanding throughout the writing process.

María Sabló-Yates

11. Telling How Long Something Has Been Happening: Hace... que: Another Use of the Present Tense

¿Cuánto tiempo hace... ? Each of the following drawings shows how long something has been going on. Stop the tape and look at the drawings. Then answer the questions. Each will be said twice.

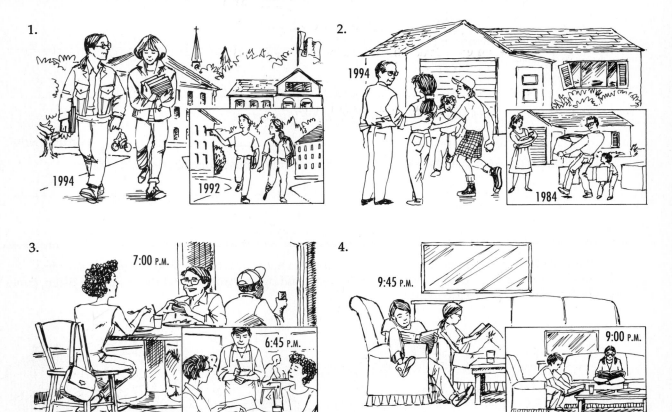

1.

1994

1992

2.

1994

1984

3.

7:00 P.M.

6:45 P.M.

4.

9:45 P.M.

9:00 P.M.

SITUACIONES

A. En una tienda de ropa. In the following conversation, you will hear how to talk to a salesperson about clothes that you are interested in purchasing. Read the dialogue silently as you listen to the speakers.

DEPENDIENTA: ¿Le atienden? ¿Qué desea?
CLIENTE: Busco un pantalón de algodón de color oscuro, para mí.
DEPENDIENTA: ¿Qué talla usa?
CLIENTE: La trece, por lo general.
DEPENDIENTA: ¿Qué le parece este pantalón negro?
CLIENTE: No está mal. Y ¿qué tal una blusa de seda también?
DEPENDIENTA: Cómo no. En su talla tenemos blusas de seda en color *beige*, rojo y gris perla. Son perfectas para este pantalón.
CLIENTE: ¿Dónde me los puedo probar?
DEPENDIENTA: Allí están los probadores. Si necesita algo, mi nombre es Méndez.
CLIENTE: Gracias.

B. En una zapatería. Now you will participate in a similar conversation, partially printed in your manual, about buying a pair of shoes. Complete the conversation, using the cues. ¡OJO! The cues are not given in sequence. (Remember to repeat the correct answer. If you wish, stop the tape and write the answers.) Here are the cues for your conversation.

Muchas gracias. / El ocho / Negros o pardos. / Busco un par de zapatos para mí.

DEPENDIENTE: Buenos días. ¿En qué puedo servirle?

UD.: Buenos días. _____

DEPENDIENTE: ¿De qué color?

UD.: _____

DEPENDIENTE: Pues, aquí tenemos de todo. ¿Qué tamaño usa?

UD.: _____ , por lo general.

DEPENDIENTE: Bueno, tome asiento (*be seated*) mientras le busco unos pares para probar.

UD.: _____

UN POCO DE TODO (PARA ENTREGAR)

A. Buscando regalos para papá. Listen to a conversation between a brother and sister, José and Ana, who need to buy a gift for their father. Do not be distracted by unfamiliar vocabulary. As you listen, circle only the items that they decide to buy.

B. *Listening Passage:* El Rastro

Antes de escuchar. Before you listen to the passage, *stop the tape* and do the following prelistening exercise.

It is sometimes helpful to answer questions about yourself that are related to a passage that you will listen to or read. Answering the following questions will give you an idea of the information the passage might contain.

1. ¿Hay un mercado al aire libre en la ciudad donde tú vives?
2. Por lo general, ¿qué venden en los mercados al aire libre?
3. ¿Cómo crees que son los precios en un mercado al aire libre?
4. ¿Te gusta ir de compras?
5. ¿Te gusta regatear?
6. ¿Coleccionas algo? ¿Sellos (*Stamps*), monedas (*coins*), libros viejos, trenes (*trains*), muñecas (*dolls*)?

Now turn on the tape.

Listening Passage. Now, you will hear a passage about El Rastro, an open-air market in Madrid. The narrator is from Spain. The following words and phrases appear in the passage.

los sellos	*stamps*
las monedas	*coins*
los domingos	*on Sundays*
los puestos	*stalls*

Después de escuchar. You will hear a series of incomplete sentences. Each will be said twice. Circle the letter of the phrase that best completes each.

1. a. una gran tienda

   b. un centro comercial

   c. un mercado con muchos puestos

2. a. todo el fin de semana

   b. el domingo por la mañana

   c. el domingo por la tarde

3. a. sólo ropa y zapatos

   b. sólo cosas para coleccionistas (*collectors*)

   c. muchas cosas de todo tipo

4. a. en Madrid y es muy famoso

   b. en España y es nuevo

   c. en todas las ciudades de España

C. ¿Qué ropa llevan estas personas? You will hear a series of questions. Answer, based on the drawings. You will describe the clothing these people are wearing and tell who they might be, where they might be, or where they might be going. Stop the tape and write the answers.

1. _____

   _____

2. _____

   _____

3. _____

   _____

D. Descripción: En casa de la familia Cárdenas. You will hear a series of statements about the drawing. Circle **C** (**cierto**) if the statement is true or **F** (**falso**) if it is false, according to the drawing. After you have listened to the statements, stop the tape and correct the false statements in the spaces provided. Before listening, stop the tape and look carefully at the drawing.

1. C F _____

2. C F _____

3. C F _____

4. C F _____

5. C F _____

6. C F _____

7. C F _____

E. Y para terminar… Entrevista: Temas varios. You will hear a series of questions. Each will be said twice. Answer, based on your own experience. No answers will be given on the tape. Stop the tape and write the answers.

1. _____

2. _____

3. _____

4. _____

5. _____

6. _____

REPASO **1**

A. Conversaciones privadas. You will overhear a conversation in which two people talk about some of their acquaintances. Then you will hear two sentences in English about the conversation. Circle the number of the statement that best describes the conversation. Try to get the gist of the conversation, and don't worry about unfamiliar vocabulary.

      1   2

B. ¿Dónde están estas personas? You will hear five brief conversations or parts of conversations. Listen carefully and next to the number of the conversation, write the location in which each conversation is taking place. First, listen to the list of possible locations.

    una casa   una clase de matemáticas
    una biblioteca   una librería
    una clase de lenguas   una fiesta estudiantil

1. _____   4. _____

2. _____   5. _____

3. _____

C. Cosas de todos los días. Practice talking about yourself and others, using the written cues. When you hear the corresponding number, form sentences using the words given in the order given, making any necessary changes and additions. You will hear the correct answer on the tape.

1. (yo) llegar / universidad / temprano, / 7:30

2. profesores / llegar / temprano / también

3. Raúl y yo / ir / biblioteca / con frecuencia

4. (nosotros) estudiar / allí / 2 / hora / todas las noches

5. Raúl / tener / un / clase / sicología / 11:00 A.M.

6. (ellos) vender / mucho / cosas / en / librería

7. (yo) ir / librería / antes de (*before*) / mi clase de computación

8. (yo) comprar / un / mochila / nuevo / por (*for*) / $40.00

D. Conversación: En la facultad (Para entregar). You will hear a conversation, partially printed in your manual, between two friends who pass each other on campus. Then you will participate in a similar conversation, playing Luisa's role. Answer, based on your own experience. No answers will be given on the tape. Stop the tape and write the answers.

ALFREDO: Hola, Luisa. ¿Qué tal?

LUISA: _____

ALFREDO: Regular. ¿Cuándo es el examen en la clase de geografía?

LUISA: _____

ALFREDO: Buena suerte (*luck*), ¿eh? ¿Tienes que trabajar en la librería hoy?

LUISA: _____

ALFREDO: Bueno, hasta luego, Luisa.

LUISA: _____

E. Descripción. You will hear a series of statements about the following cartoon. Each will be said twice. Circle **C (cierto)** if the statement is true or **F (falso)** if it is false. First, stop the tape and look at the cartoon.

1. C F   2. C F   3. C F   4. C F   5. C F   6. C F

F. Descripción: De compras en el mercado. You will hear a series of statements about the following drawing. Each will be said twice. Circle **C** (**cierto**) if the statement is true or **F** (**falso**) if it is false. First, stop the tape and look at the drawing.

1. C F   2. C F   3. C F   4. C F   5. C F

G. Entrevista: Temas diversos (Para entregar). You will hear a series of questions about yourself. Each will be said twice. Answer, based on your own experience. No answers will be given on the tape. Stop the tape and write the answers.

1. _____

2. _____

3. _____

4. _____

5. _____

6. _____

7. _____

8. _____

CAPÍTULO **4**

VOCABULARIO: PREPARACIÓN

A. Dictado: El horario de la profesora Velásquez. Imagine that you are Professor Velásquez's secretary and that you are filling in her weekly calendar. Listen carefully as she tells you her schedule for this week, and fill in the blanks in the calendar. Some of the entries have already been made. First, stop the tape and look at the calendar.

lunes	martes	miércoles	jueves	viernes
mañana 10:45 AM : Clase de conversación	mañana _____ : dentista	mañana _____ :	mañana _____ :	mañana _____ :
tarde _____ :	tarde _____ :	tarde _____ :	tarde 3:00PM : Clase de español	tarde _____ :

B. Definiciones. You will hear a series of definitions. Each will be said twice. Write the number of the definition next to the location described. First, listen to the list of locations.

___ una alcoba   ___ una sala

___ un comedor   ___ una cocina

___ un patio

C. **¿Qué hay en esta sala?** You will hear the names of a series of items. Say the number to which each corresponds; then repeat the name. Follow the model.

MODELO: (*you hear*) una mesa → (*you say*) El número seis es una mesa.

1. ... 2. ... 3. ... 4. ... 5. ... 6. ...

D. **¿Qué hacemos los viernes por la noche?** Practice telling what you and your friends do on Friday nights. Use the written and oral cues.

1. Marisol
2. Armando y Elena
3. yo

4. mi hermana y yo
5. tú

E. **Situaciones.** You will hear a series of situations. Choose the best response or solution to each from the following list. First, listen to the list.

hacer una pregunta
poner el radio
poner el televisor

salir para la biblioteca
hacer un viaje a España
salir del comedor y entrar en la sala

MODELO: (*you hear*) Me gusta el programa «In Living Color». →
(*you say*) Por eso pongo el televisor.

1. ... 2. ... 3. ... 4. ... 5. ...

F. **Preguntas.** You will hear a series of questions. Each will be said twice. Answer in the affirmative or negative, as indicated.

1. Sí, ...
2. Sí, ...
3. Sí, ...

4. No, no...
5. No, no...

LOS HISPANOS HABLAN: DICTADO: ¿QUÉ COSAS TIENES EN TU HABITACIÓN?

This question is answered by Xiomara. As you listen to the passage, jot down some of the things that she has in her room. The following words appear in the passage.

el abanico	*fan*
el tocador	*dressing table*
los cuadros	pinturas
la gata de peluche	*stuffed toy cat*
me regaló	*he gave me* (*as a gift*)
el novio	*boyfriend*

Lo que Xiomara tiene en su habitación:

_____

_____

_____

_____

PRONUNCIACIÓN Y ORTOGRAFÍA: **B/V**

Spanish **b** and **v** are pronounced exactly the same way. At the beginning of a phrase, or after **m** or **n, b** and **v** are pronounced like the English *b*, as a stop; that is, no air is allowed to escape through the lips. In all other positions, **b** and **v** are fricatives; that is, they are produced by allowing some air to escape through the lips. There is no equivalent for this sound in English.

A. Repeat the following words and phrases, imitating the speaker. Note that the type of *b* sound you will hear is indicated at the beginning of the series.

1. [b]   bueno   viejo   verde   barato   baño   hombre
2. [ƀ]   llevar   libro   pobre   abrigo   universidad   abuelo
3. [b/ƀ]   bueno / es bueno   busca / Ud. busca   bien / muy bien   en Venezuela / de Venezuela vende / se vende
4. [b/ƀ]   beber   bebida   vivir   biblioteca   Babel   vívido

B. Dictado. You will hear four sentences. Each will be said twice. Listen carefully and write what you hear.

1. _____

2. _____

3. _____

4. _____

12. Expressing Actions: Present Tense of Stem-Changing Verbs

A. Minidiálogo: ¡Por fin salieron! You will hear a dialogue followed by a series of statements. Next to each of the following statements, write the letter of the person who might have made the statement.

a = Miguel   b = Alicia

1. ___ No quiero hablar de política.

2. ___ No me gustan tus amigos.

3. ___ ¡Tú exageras mucho!

4. ___ ¡Tú juegas muy mal a las cartas!

B. Encuesta. You will hear a series of statements about your habits. For each statement, check the appropriate response. No answers will be given on the tape. The answers you choose should be correct for you!

	SIEMPRE	CON FRECUENCIA	A VECES	¡NUNCA!
1.	☐	☐	☐	☐
2.	☐	☐	☐	☐
3.	☐	☐	☐	☐
4.	☐	☐	☐	☐
5.	☐	☐	☐	☐
6.	☐	☐	☐	☐
7.	☐	☐	☐	☐
8.	☐	☐	☐	☐

C. Un sábado típico en mi casa. Tell about the activities of your fictitious family on a typical Saturday. Use the written and oral cues.

1. yo
2. mi hermano
3. mis padres
4. mi hermana y yo
5. tú
6. el perro y el gato

D. Entrevista con los señores Ruiz. Interview Mr. and Mrs. Ruiz about some of the things they like to do. Use the written cues. You will hear an answer to your questions on the tape. Remember to repeat the correct question.

MODELO: (*you hear*) jugar al tenis →
(*you say*) ¿Juegan al tenis? (*you hear*) No, no jugamos al tenis.

1. ...   2. ...   3. ...   4. ...

13. Expressing *-self/-selves:* Reflexive Pronouns

A. Dictado: Minidiálogo: Un día típico. You will hear the following description of a typical day in the life of Alicia and Miguel. Listen carefully and complete the description. Then, you will hear a series of statements about the description. Circle **C** if the statement is true or **F** if it is false.

___ llamo Alicia; mi esposo ___ llama Miguel. ___ despierto y ___ levanto temprano, a las seis. Él

también ___ levanta temprano. ___ bañamos y ___ vestimos. Luego, yo pongo la mesa y él prepara el

desayuno. ¡Por fin! Estamos listos para salir para la oficina. Pero… un momentito. ¡Es un día feriado!

¿Es demasiado tarde para acostar___ otra vez? No, pero… desgraciadamente, ¡ya no tenemos sueño!

1. C F Alicia y su esposo se levantan temprano.

2. C F Miguel prepara el desayuno.

3. C F Alicia y Miguel trabajan los días feriados.

B. Encuesta. You will hear a series of statements about your habits. For each statement, check the appropriate response. No answers will be given on the tape. The answers you choose should be correct for you!

	SIEMPRE	CON FRECUENCIA	A VECES	¡NUNCA!
1.	□	□	□	□
2.	□	□	□	□
3.	□	□	□	□
4.	□	□	□	□
5.	□	□	□	□
6.	□	□	□	□
7.	□	□	□	□
8.	□	□	□	□

C. Hábitos y costumbres. Practice telling about some of the habits of the members of your fictitious family. Use the oral and written cues.

1. yo
2. mi primo y yo
3. tú
4. mi hermanito
5. mis abuelos
6. mi madre

14. Expressing Possession: Possessive Adjectives (Unstressed)

A. ¿Cuál es su casa? You will hear a description of Alicia and Miguel's house, read by Alicia. Listen to the description and circle the number of the drawing that matches the description.

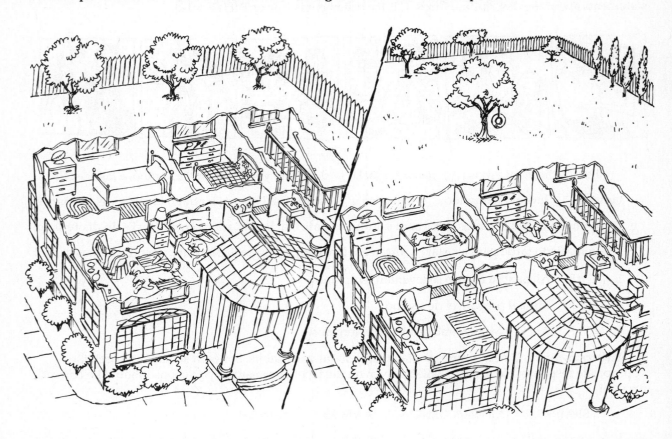

B. ¿Cómo es el apartamento de Vicente? Practice describing Vicente's apartment, using the oral and written cues. Remember to change the endings of the adjectives, if necessary.

> MODELO: (*you hear*) apartamento   (*you see*) pequeño → (*you say*) Su apartamento es pequeño.

1. pequeño también
2. cómodo, pero pequeño
3. amplio
4. viejo
5. blanco

C. ¡Qué confusión! Sara asks you to clarify what belongs to whom. You will hear each question twice. Answer, according to the model.

> MODELO: (*you hear*) ¿Es la casa de Paco? → (*you say*) No, no es su casa.

1. …   2. …   3. …   4. …   5. …

D. Preguntas: Hablando de muebles. You will hear a series of questions about where certain pieces of furniture are located in your family's house. Answer, using the written cues.

> MODELO: (*you hear*) ¿Dónde está su cama?   (*you see*) alcoba →
> (*you say*) Nuestra cama está en la alcoba.

1. sala   2. patio   3. comedor   4. cocina / y / alcoba

15. Pointing Out People and Things: Demonstrative Adjectives

A. Dictado: Minidiálogo: Cuando hay muchos invitados. You will hear a dialogue about sleeping arrangements at Jorge's house. Listen carefully and complete the dialogue. Then, you will hear a series of statements. Circle **C** if the statement is true or **F** if it is false.

JORGE: Hombre, lo siento. No hay _____ para todos, con tantas _____ en casa.

MIGUEL: No importa. Pero, dime, ¿dónde puedo dormir_____ _____?

JORGE: Bueno, _____ _____ grande es muy cómodo. Ah, también tenemos

_____ hamaca en el _____. Pero yo realmente te recomiendo _____

_____. Es viejo, pero cómodo.

1. C F   Hay muchas personas en casa de Jorge esta noche.

2. C F   El sillón y el sofá son cómodos.

3. C F   El sofá está en el patio.

B. ¿Cómo son estas cosas? Answer, using the oral cues and an appropriate form of the indicated demonstrative adjective. Remember to change the endings of the adjectives, and use **es** or **son,** as appropriate.

MODELO: *(you see)* ese / sofás   *(you hear)* verde → *(you say)* Esos sofás son verdes.

1. ese / armario
2. este / pantalones
3. aquel / cómoda
4. este / faldas
5. ese / sillones

C. Recuerdos de su viaje a México. Your friends want to know all about your trip to Mexico. Answer their questions, using an appropriate form of the demonstrative adjective **aquel** and the oral cues.

MODELO: *(you hear and see)* ¿Qué tal el restaurante El Charro?   *(you hear)* excelente →
        (you say) ¡Aquel restaurante es excelente!

1. ¿Qué tal el hotel Libertad?
2. ¿Y los dependientes del hotel?
3. ¿Qué tal la ropa *(clothing)* en el Mercado de la Merced?
4. ¿Y los parques de la capital?

D. Situaciones. You will hear a series of situations. Circle the letter of the best reaction to each.

1. a. ¡Esto es terrible!   b. ¡Esto es magnífico!

2. a. ¡Eso es terrible!   b. ¡Eso es magnífico!

3. a. ¡Eso es terrible!   b. ¡Eso es magnífico!

4. a. ¡Eso es terrible!   b. ¡Eso es magnífico!

SITUACIONES

A. La rutina diaria. In the following conversation, you will hear ways to generalize about the life you lead. Read the dialogue silently as you listen to the speakers.

LILIANA: ¿Qué tal, Horacio? ¿Cómo va tu semestre?
HORACIO: ¿La verdad? Llevo una vida muy aburrida.
LILIANA: ¡No seas tan pesimista! Eso siempre pasa al final del semestre, ¿no?
HORACIO: Sí, pero ahora es fatal. Hago las mismas cosas todos los días. Tengo clases de las ocho a las dos. Después voy a la biblioteca y hago todos mis deberes. A las seis empiezo a trabajar en un restaurante y salgo a las diez. Por suerte tengo libres los jueves, que es cuando voy de compras o a la lavandería. Cuando llego a casa, estoy agotado. Leo un rato y… a dormir.
LILIANA: ¿A qué hora te levantas, por lo general?
HORACIO: No lo vas a creer, pero me levanto a las seis todos los días. Hago un poco de ejercicio, me baño, tomo el desayuno, arreglo mi cuarto y me preparo el desayuno. ¡Qué ganas tengo de empezar a trabajar y no estudiar más!

B. Conversación. Now you will participate in a similar conversation, partially printed in your manual, about your daily routine. You will take the role of Roberto. Complete the conversation, using the following cues. **¡OJO!** The cues are not listed in order. First, listen to the cues.

de ocho a cinco   muy ocupada
después de trabajar   ir de compras o leer el periódico

MARTA: Hola, Roberto. ¿Qué hay de nuevo?

ROBERTO: Pues, últimamente, llevo una vida _____.

MARTA: Y eso, ¿por qué?

ROBERTO: Bueno, tengo un trabajo nuevo. Estoy en la oficina _____.

_____, asisto a clases de noche en la universidad. Casi no

tengo tiempo para _____.

MARTA: Bueno, hombre, a ver si las cosas se calman un poco.

ROBERTO: Gracias, pero lo dudo.

UN POCO DE TODO (PARA ENTREGAR)

A. Dictado: La rutina diaria de Elvira. You will hear the following series of incomplete statements about Elvira's daily routine. Each will be said once. As you listen, write in the missing information. Then, stop the tape and put the sentences in chronological order.

a. ___ En la oficina, _____ muchas llamadas por teléfono.

b. ___ Regreso a casa agotada. _____ en el sofá y

_____ el televisor.

c. ___ Me despierto a las _____.

d. ___ Me visto y voy a _____.

e. ___ Escucho la radio _____ levantarme.

f. ___ A _____, me pongo el pijama y me acuesto.

g. ___ _____ el desayuno.

h. ___ Por fin me levanto y me _____.

i. ___ Salgo para _____.

j. ___ Después de trabajar _____ horas, salgo a cenar con

_____.

k. ___ Leo el periódico _____ desayunar.

After you have put the sentences in chronological order, turn on the tape.

B. *Listening Passage:* Susana habla de su familia y de sus estudios

Primera parte

Antes de escuchar. Before you listen to the first part of the passage, *stop the tape* and do the following prelistening exercises.

Paso 1. Read the following true/false statements. As you read them, try to infer the information the passage will give you, as well as the specific information for which you need to listen.

1. Susana es española.
2. La familia de Susana vive en Madrid.
3. Susana tiene hermanos, pero no tiene sobrinos.
4. Hay otra persona en la familia de Susana que también se llama Susana.
5. En los países hispanos existe la tradición de ponerles a los hijos los nombres de los padres o de otros parientes.

Paso 2. Now, based on the true/false statements, indicate the topics that you think might be covered in the listening passage.

☐ Susana might tell us her nationality or where she is from.

☐ She might tell us where her favorite professor lives.

☐ She will probably tell us something about her family.

☐ She might tell us about certain customs relating to the naming of children in Hispanic countries.

Now turn on the tape.

Listening Passage (1). Now you will hear the first part of the passage. In this part, Julia's friend Susana will tell you about her family. Julia told you a bit about Susana when she introduced herself in the listening passage in **Ante todo.** Do you remember where Susana is from?

Después de escuchar. Here are the true/false statements. Circle **C** if the statement is true or **F** if it is false. Then correct the statements that are false, according to the passage.

1. C   F   Susana es española.

   _____

2. C   F   La familia de Susana vive en Madrid.

   _____

3. C   F   Susana tiene hermanos, pero no tiene sobrinos.

   _____

4. C   F   Hay otra persona en la familia de Susana que también se llama Susana.

   _____

5. C   F   En los países hispanos existe la tradición de ponerles a los hijos los nombres de los padres
            o de otros parientes.

   _____

Now turn on the tape.

Segunda parte

Antes de escuchar. *Stop the tape,* and read the following questions about the second part of the listening passage. As you read them, try to infer the information the passage will give you, as well as the specific information for which you need to listen.

1. ¿Por qué estudia Susana en España?
2. ¿Con quién vive?
3. ¿Qué aspecto de la vida es similar en España y en el Paraguay?
4. ¿Qué *no* hacen los españoles?
5. Para muchos hispanos, ¿es normal tener parientes «al otro lado (*on the other side*) del Atlántico»?

Now turn on the tape.

Listening Passage (2). Now you will hear the second part of the passage. In this part, Susana will talk about her studies in Spain and tell you more about her family.

Después de escuchar. Now you will hear a series of questions about the second listening passage. Each will be said twice. Circle the letter of the best response to each.

1. a.   Porque en España hay muchas universidades y porque algunos de sus parientes viven allí.

   b.   Porque las universidades del Paraguay no son buenas.

2. a.   Vive con otros estudiantes paraguayos, en una residencia estudiantil.

   b.   Vive con su tía y su abuela.

3. a.   La vida familiar es similar en ambos (*both*) países.

   b.   No hay ninguna semejanza (*similarity*) entre los dos países.

4. a. No hablan guaraní.

   b. No visitan a sus parientes en Latinoamérica.

5. a. No, no es normal.

   b. Sí, es normal.

C. Entrevista. You will hear a series of questions. Each will be said twice. Answer, based on your own experience. No answers will be given on the tape. Stop the tape and write the answers.

1. _____

2. _____

3. _____

4. _____

5. _____

6. _____

7. _____

D. Y para terminar... En el periódico: Pisos y apartamentos. The housing ads on the next page appeared in a Spanish newspaper. Look at the descriptions of the apartments and decide which one you are most interested in. Then answer the questions you will hear. Each will be said twice. If the ad for the apartment you have chosen doesn't contain the information requested in the questions, say **No lo dice.** No answers will be given on the tape. Stop the tape and write the answers. First, listen to the list of new words.

el alquiler   *rent*
la dirección   *address*

Now stop the tape and look at the ads.

1. _____

2. _____

3. _____

4. _____

5. _____

6. _____

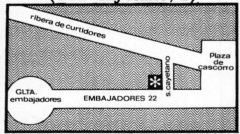

CAPÍTULO **5**

VOCABULARIO: PREPARACIÓN

A. ¿Qué tiempo hace? You will hear a series of weather conditions. Each will be said twice. Give the number of the drawing to which each corresponds, then repeat the description. First, stop the tape and look at the drawings.

1.

2.

3.

4.

5.

B. ¿Cuándo es... ? Your Peruvian friend Evangelina wants to know when certain events take place, including a birth date, **una fecha de nacimiento,** an anniversary, **un aniversario,** and a national holiday, **una fiesta nacional.** Answer, using the written cues.

MODELO: (*you hear*) ¿Cuándo es el cumpleaños de Nicolás? (*you see*) Sunday, May 4 →
(*you say*) Es el domingo, cuatro de mayo.

1. Friday, August 10
2. Saturday, November 22
3. Wednesday, April 14

4. February 11, 1899
5. July 4, 1776

C. El tiempo y las actividades. You will hear a series of weather conditions. Respond with activities that are appropriate for them. Begin each sentence with **Por eso...** and use the **yo** form of the verbs. First, listen to the list of activities.

ponerse el impermeable ir a las montañas (*mountains*)
no salir de casa ponerse una camiseta y pantalones cortos
ponerse un suéter

MODELO: (*you hear*) Hace mucho frío hoy. → (*you say*) Por eso me pongo un suéter.

1. ... 2. ... 3. ... 4. ...

D. ¿Dónde está? You will hear a series of descriptions. Listen carefully and name the country or location described. You will be listening for specific information about the location of the place or item.

1. ... 2. ... 3. ...

4. ... 5. ... 6. ...

LOS HISPANOS HABLAN: DINOS ALGO ACERCA DE TU ESCUELA

You will hear three brief answers highlighting aspects of school life in Hispanic countries. Students who answer represent Spain, Argentina, and Costa Rica. As you listen, check the boxes that indicate what the speakers say about their countries. First, stop the tape and look at the information for which you need to listen.

	SÍ	NO	
España			
1.	☐	☐	La escuela está bastante (*fairly*) cerca de casa.
2.	☐	☐	Llevan uniforme.
3.	☐	☐	Almuerzan en la escuela.
la Argentina			
1.	☐	☐	La escuela está bastante cerca de casa.
2.	☐	☐	Llevan uniforme.
3.	☐	☐	Almuerzan en la escuela.
Costa Rica			
1.	☐	☐	La escuela está bastante cerca de casa.
2.	☐	☐	Llevan uniforme.
3.	☐	☐	Almuerzan en la escuela.

Now turn on the tape.

PRONUNCIACIÓN Y ORTOGRAFÍA: **R** *AND* **RR**

The letter **r** has two pronunciations in Spanish: the trilled **r** (written as **rr** between vowels or as **r** at the beginning of a word), and the flap **r**, which appears in all other positions. Because mispronunciations can alter the meaning of a word, it is important to distinguish between these two pronunciations of the Spanish **r**. For example: **coro** (*chorus*) and **corro** (*I run*).

The flap **r** is similar to the sound produced by the rapid pronunciation of *tt* and *dd* in the English words *Betty* and *ladder*.

A. Listen to these word pairs. Then repeat them.

petty / pero *sadder* / Sara *motor* / moro

B. Repeat the following words, phrases, and sentences, imitating the speaker.

1. arte gracias para vender triste

2. ruso Roberto real reportero rebelde

3. burro corral carro barra corro

4. el nombre correcto el precio del cuaderno las residencias Enrique, Carlos y Rosita

una mujer refinada el extranjero Puerto Rico Busco un carro caro.

Soy el primo de Roberto Ramírez. Estos errores son raros.

C. *¿R o rr?* You will hear a series of words. Each will be said twice. Circle the letter of the word you hear.

1. a. ahora   b. ahorra   4. a. coral   b. corral

2. a. caro   b. carro   5. a. pero   b. perro

3. a. coro   b. corro

D. Trabalenguas. You will hear the following Spanish tongue-twister. Listen to it once, then repeat it, imitating the speaker.

> R con R guitarra.
> R con R barril.
> Mira qué rápido corren (*run*)
> los carros del ferrocarril (*railroad*).

MINIDIÁLOGOS Y GRAMÁTICA

16. *¿Ser o estar?* Summary of the Uses of **ser** and **estar**

A. Minidiálogo: Un viaje de invierno. You will hear a dialogue, followed by a series of statements. Circle **C** if the statement is true or **F** if it is false.

1. C F   Los dos hombres van a Cancún.

2. C F   Hace mucho frío en Cancún en invierno.

3. C F   Liliana, la esposa de Carlos, trabaja mucho.

4. C F   Los dos hombres son amigos, probablemente.

B. ¿Qué pregunta hiciste? (*What question did you ask?*) You will hear a series of statements that contain **ser** or **estar**. Each will be said twice. Circle the letter of the question that corresponds to each.

1. a. ¿Cómo estás?   b. ¿Cómo eres?

2. a. ¿Cómo están?   b. ¿Cómo son?

3. a. ¿Dónde estás?   b. ¿De dónde eres?

4. a. ¿Dónde está el carro?   b. ¿De dónde es el carro?

5. a. ¿De quién es la alfombra?   b. ¿De qué es la alfombra?

C. Marcos, ¿qué tal? Tell how your friend Marcos seems to be feeling on these different occasions, using one of these adjectives. Use Marcos's name only in the first sentence. First, listen to the list of adjectives.

nervioso   furioso   triste   contento   preocupado

1.

2.

3.

4.

5.

1. ...   2. ...   3. ...   4. ...   5. ...

D. Opuestos. You will hear a series of questions. Each will be said twice. Answer in the negative.

MODELO: (*you hear*) ¿Está limpia la mesa? → (*you say*) No. Está sucia.

1. ...   2. ...   3. ...   4. ...   5. ...   6. ...

E. ¿Quiénes son? Imagine that the people in this photograph are your relatives. Tell who they are and describe them, using the oral cues and the appropriate forms of **ser** or **estar.** The first question is about the couple on the right. Begin your answer to that question with **Son...**

1. ...   2. ...   3. ...   4. ...   5. ...   6. ...

F. Una fiesta para los estudiantes extranjeros. You have called your friend Susana from a party, and she cannot understand what you are saying. Answer her questions in the affirmative, using **ser** or **estar** as appropriate.

> MODELO: (*you hear*) ¿Tú? ¿Muy cansado hoy? → (*you say*) Sí, estoy muy cansado hoy.

1. ... 2. ... 3. ... 4. ...

17. Describing: Comparisons

A. Minidiálogo: Tipos y estereotipos. You will hear a brief description of the people in the following drawing. Then you will hear a series of statements about them. Circle **C** if the statement is true or **F** if it is false.

1. C F   Adolfo es más extrovertido que Raúl.

2. C F   Raúl es menos estudioso que Adolfo.

3. C F   Adolfo tiene tantas clases como Raúl.

4. C F   Esteban tiene menos amigos que Raúl.

B. La rutina de Alicia. The following chart shows Alicia's routine for weekdays and weekends. You will hear a series of statements about the chart. Each will be said twice. Circle **C** if the statement is true or **F** if it is false, according to the chart. First stop the tape and read the chart.

ACCIÓN	DE LUNES A VIERNES	SÁBADO Y DOMINGO
levantarse	6:30	9:30
desayunar	7:15	10:00
trabajar	8 horas	1 hora
almorzar	20 minutos	30 minutos
divertirse	1 hora	8 horas
acostarse	11:00	11:00

1. C F   2. C F   3. C F   4. C F   5. C F

C. Un desacuerdo. You and your friend Lourdes don't agree on anything! React to her statements negatively, following the model and using the written cues.

> MODELO: (*you hear and see*) La amistad (*friendship*) es más importante que el amor.
> (*you see*) tan → (*you say*) ¡No! La amistad es tan importante como el amor.

1. Hace tanto calor en el desierto (*desert*) como en las montañas. (más)

2. La temperatura es más alta en invierno que en verano. (menos)

3. La clase de cálculo es menos difícil que la clase de química. (tan)

4. Los niños esperan más pacientemente que los adultos. (menos)

D. Un acuerdo perfecto. Rafael and Carmen always do and have the same things. Describe their relationship, using the oral cues.

> MODELO: (*you hear*) beber / café → (*you say*) Rafael bebe tanto café como Carmen.

1. ... 2. ... 3. ... 4. ...

18. Getting Information: Summary of Interrogative Words

A. Preguntas y respuestas. You will hear a series of questions. Each will be said twice. Circle the letter of the best answer to each.

1.	a. Es de Juan.	b.	Es negro.
2.	a. Están en México.	b.	Son de México.
3.	a. Soy alto y delgado.	b.	Bien, gracias. ¿Y Ud.?
4.	a. Mañana.	b.	Tengo cinco.
5.	a. Es gris.	b.	Tengo frío.
6.	a. Con Elvira.	b.	Elvira va a la tienda.
7.	a. A las nueve.	b.	Son las nueve.

B. ¿Qué dijiste? (*What did you say?*) Your friend Eva has just made several statements, but you haven't understood everything she said. You will hear each statement only once. Choose an appropriate interrogative word and form a question to elicit the information you need.

> MODELO: (*you hear*) Llegan mañana. (*you see*) a. ¿dónde? b. ¿cuándo? →
> (*you say*) b. ¿Cuándo llegan?

1.	a. ¿de quién?	b.	¿quién?
2.	a. ¿quiénes?	b.	¿qué?
3.	a. ¿de dónde?	b.	¿adónde?
4.	a. ¿cuál?	b.	¿qué?
5.	a. ¿cuántos?	b.	¿cuánto?
6.	a. ¿a qué hora?	b.	¿qué hora es?

C. Entrevista con la señorita Moreno. Interview Ms. Moreno, an exchange student, for your campus newspaper, using the written cues. Add any necessary words. You will hear the correct question, as well as her answer.

> MODELO: (*you see*) ¿dónde? / ser →
> (*you say*) Srta. Moreno, ¿de dónde es Ud.? (*you hear*) Soy de Chile.

1. ¿dónde? / vivir
2. ¿dónde? / trabajar
3. ¿qué? / idiomas / hablar

4. ¿qué? / instrumento / tocar
5. ¿cuál? / ser / deporte favorito

19. Talking About the Past (1): Some Forms of the Preterite

A. Minidiálogo: ¿Qué hizo Ricardo ayer?

Paso 1. You will hear the following description of what Ricardo Maldonado did yesterday. Look at the drawings and read the description silently as you listen.

Paso 2. Now you will hear the description a second time. Repeat each phrase or sentence after you hear it.

B. Encuesta: Hablando de lo que hiciste ayer. (*Speaking about what you did yesterday.*) You will hear a series of statements about what you did yesterday. For each statement, check the appropriate answer. The answers you choose should be correct for you!

1. ☐ Sí ☐ No
2. ☐ Sí ☐ No
3. ☐ Sí ☐ No
4. ☐ Sí ☐ No

5. ☐ Sí ☐ No
6. ☐ Sí ☐ No
7. ☐ Sí ☐ No

C. **¿Quién lo hizo?** You will hear a series of questions about what your friends did last night, **anoche.** Each will be said twice. Answer according to the drawings. First, stop the tape and look at the drawings.

MODELO: (*you hear*) ¿Quién habló por teléfono?... → (*you say*) Alicia habló por teléfono.

SITUACIONES

Pronóstico del tiempo. You will hear a conversation about plans for a trip and how the weather affects them. Read the conversation silently as you listen. Then you will hear a series of statements about the conversation. Circle **C** if the statement is true or **F** if it is false.

—Oye, ¿sabes qué tiempo va a hacer en San Sebastián la próxima semana? ¿Qué dice la televisión?
—Supongo que fresco, pero no estoy seguro. Nunca miro la tele para saber qué tiempo hace. No confío en sus predicciones.
—Fantástico, pero... ¿qué ropa debo llevar? Es la primera vez que voy a San Sebastián. Tú, ¿qué crees?
—En diciembre hace frío en toda España, pero San Sebastián está en la costa.
—¿Y qué?
—Pues que la temperatura es siempre más suave. Lleva una buena chaqueta y un impermeable. Llueve bastante.
—¿Estás seguro? Sólo tengo una hora para hacer la maleta. El tren sale a las siete.
—No te preocupes. En cuanto a las predicciones sobre el tiempo, tengo razón con más frecuencia que la tele.

(*Más tarde, en el tren, en la radio*)

«Como ya se comunicó en anteriores servicios informativos, un frente frío de gran intensidad azota las costas del norte. La nieve sigue cayendo en Bilbao y San Sebastián y esta noche se espera que las temperaturas bajarán a un grado bajo cero.»

1. C F   2. C F   3. C F   4. C F

UN POCO DE TODO (PARA ENTREGAR)

A. En el periódico: Hablando del clima. Look at the following chart of temperatures from a Spanish newspaper from October. Then answer the questions you will hear about the chart. You will hear each question twice. Stop the tape and write the answers. First, listen to the list of symbols.

A = agradable	f = frío	Q = cubierto (*cloudy*)
C = mucho calor	H = heladas (*frost*)	S = tormentas
c = calor	N = nevadas	T = templado (*mild*)
D = despejado (*clear*)	P = lluvioso	V = vientos fuertes (*strong*)
F = mucho frío		

Now stop the tape and scan the chart.

TEMPERATURAS		MÁX.	MÍN.
Ámsterdam	D	12	4
Atenas	D	22	15
Barcelona	D	21	14
Berlín	Q	8	6
Bonn	Q	14	2
Bruselas	D	12	2
Buenos Aires	Q	17	12
Cairo, El	D	26	18
Caracas	D	26	20
Copenhague	D	9	3
Dublín	Q	12	8
Estocolmo	f	7	6
Francfort	Q	11	4
Ginebra	Q	13	11
Hamburgo	Q	8	6
Lisboa	D	19	13
Londres	D	13	1
Madrid	A	20	10
México	Q	25	10
Miami	Q	27	23
Moscú	D	2	–6
Munich	f	8	7
Nueva York	D	19	9
Oslo	f	8	4
París	D	13	5
Rabat	Q	23	18
R. de Janeiro	P	25	20
Roma	D	23	15
Tokio	Q	17	12
Viena	Q	12	10
Zurich	Q	16	9

1. _____

2. _____

3. _____

4. _____

5. _____

B. *Listening Passage:* **Hablando del clima**

Antes de escuchar. Before you listen to the passage, *stop the tape* and do the following prelistening exercises.

Paso 1. Read the following true/false statements. As you read them, try to infer the information the passage will give you, as well as the specific information for which you need to listen.

1. En las regiones tropicales, por lo general, hay una estación seca (*dry*) y una lluviosa (*rainy*).
2. En Latinoamérica, no hace frío en ninguna región.
3. Hay climas muy variados en el mundo hispano.
4. En Sudamérica, las estaciones del año son opuestas a las (*those*) de los países del Hemisferio Norte.

Paso 2. You probably do know quite a bit about the climate in most of Latin America. That information will be fairly easy for you to recognize in the listening passage. Read the next set of true/false statements, and try to infer what type of information you need to listen for regarding the person who will narrate the passage.

La persona que habla...

1. es de Vermont.
2. prefiere el frío del invierno.
3. no sabe (*doesn't know how to*) esquiar.
4. quiere vivir en Los Andes.

A la persona que habla...

5. le molestan (*bother*) las estaciones lluviosas en los países tropicales.

Now turn on the tape.

Listening Passage. Now, you will hear a passage about the climate in different regions of the Hispanic world. This passage is read by Nicanor, a friend of Susana's. The following words appear in the passage.

seca	*dry*
lluviosa	*rainy*
molestan	*bother*
yo lo tengo claro	*it's clear to me*

Después de escuchar. Here is another version of the true/false statements you did in **Antes de leer.** Circle **C** if the statement is true or **F** if it is false. Then correct the statements that are false, according to the passage.

1. C F   Nicanor es de Vermont.

   _____

2. C F   A Nicanor no le gusta el invierno.

   _____

3. C F   En el mundo hispano, hay climas muy variados.

   _____

4. C F   En Sudamérica no hace frío en ninguna región.

   _____

5. C F   A Nicanor le gustaría (*would like*) vivir en los Andes.

   _____

6. C F   Cuando es verano en el Hemisferio Norte, también es verano en el Hemisferio Sur.

   _____

Now turn on the tape.

C. Y para terminar... Entrevista. You will hear a series of questions. Each will be said twice. Answer, based on your experience. No answers will be given on the tape. Stop the tape and write the answers.

1. _____
2. _____
3. _____
4. _____
5. _____
6. _____

CAPÍTULO **6**

VOCABULARIO: PREPARACIÓN

A.   ¿Qué va a pedir Juan? Juan and his friend Marta are in a restaurant. Listen to their conversation and circle the items that Juan is going to order. In this exercise, you will practice listening for specific information. First, stop the tape and look at the drawing.

B.   Identificaciones. Identify the following foods when you hear the corresponding number. Use the definite article in your answer.

C. Categorías. You will hear a series of words. Repeat each word, telling in what category it belongs: **un tipo de carne, un marisco, una fruta, una verdura, un postre, una bebida,** or **un tipo de pescado.**

> MODELO: (*you hear*) el té → (*you say*) El té es una bebida.

1. ... 2. ... 3. ... 4. ... 5. ... 6. ... 7. ...

D. ¡No vamos a volver a ese restaurante! You and some friends are at a restaurant, and everything is going wrong. Describe what is happening, using the oral and written cues.

1. tener mucha hambre
2. no traer el agua
3. no ver bien el menú

4. no oír bien por el ruido
5. no traer la cuenta
6. no traer dinero

E. ¿Qué acabo de hacer? Guess what your friend has just done, based on where he is. First, listen to the list of actions.

estacionar (*to park*) el coche
acostarse
hacer una pregunta

bañarse
hacer un sándwich
almorzar con unos amigos

> MODELO: (*you hear*) Estoy en una cafetería. → (*you say*) Acabas de almorzar con unos amigos.

1. ... 2. ... 3. ... 4. ... 5. ...

F. Preguntas. You will hear a series of questions. Each will be said twice. Answer, using the written cues.

1. el restaurante La Gaviota
2. una hamburguesa con papas fritas
3. en casa de una amiga

4. una ensalada de camarones
5. en mi restaurante favorito

LOS HISPANOS HABLAN: ¿QUÉ TE GUSTA MUCHO COMER?

Paso 1. In this passage, Clara tells about two dishes typical of Spain: **el cocido** and **el gazpacho.** Then you will hear a series of statements. Circle **C** if the statement is true or **F** if it is false. The following words appear in the passage.

el hueso de codillo   *leg bone (as in ham)*
la morcilla   *blood sausage*
el pepino   *cucumber*
el ajo   *garlic*
el aceite de oliva   *olive oil*
el vinagre   *vinegar*
echar por encima   *to sprinkle on top*
trocitos   *little bits (pieces)*

1. C F   2. C F   3. C F   4. C F

Paso 2. ¿Qué no te gusta nada comer? You will hear answers to this question from Clara, Xiomara, and Teresa. As they describe the foods that they do not like, check the appropriate boxes. First, listen to the list of foods.

		CLARA	XIOMARA	TERESA
1.	huevos	☐	☐	☐
2.	verduras	☐	☐	☐
3.	oreja de cerdo (*pig's ear*)	☐	☐	☐
4.	mondongo (*tripe soup*)	☐	☐	☐
5.	hamburguesas	☐	☐	☐
6.	caracoles (*snails*)	☐	☐	☐
7.	comida rápida	☐	☐	☐
8.	mantequilla (*butter*)	☐	☐	☐
9.	platos sofisticados	☐	☐	☐

Check your answers in the Appendix before you begin **Paso 3.**

Paso 3. Now you will hear a series of questions about the chart. Each will be said twice. Answer with the correct person's name. You will hear a full-sentence answer on the tape.

1. …   2. …   3. …   4. …

PRONUNCIACIÓN Y ORTOGRAFÍA: **C, QU**

A. The [k] sound in Spanish can be written two ways: before the vowels **a, o,** and **u** it is written as **c;** before **i** and **e,** it is written as **qu.** The letter **k** itself appears only in words that are borrowed from other languages. Unlike the English [k] sound, the Spanish sound is not aspirated; that is, no air is allowed to escape when it is pronounced. Compare the following pairs of English words in which the first [k] sound is aspirated and the second is not.

can / scan   cold / scold   kit / skit

B. Repeat the following words, imitating the speaker. Remember to pronounce the [k] sound without aspiration.

1.	casa	cosa	rico	loca	roca	comida	pescado	camarones
2.	¿quién?	Quito	aquí	¿qué?	pequeño	porque	paquete	quiero
3.	kilo	kilogramo	kiosco	kerosén	kilómetro	karate		

C. Read the following sentences when you hear the corresponding number. Then repeat each sentence, imitating the speaker. Pay close attention to intonation.

1. ¿Quién quiere comer en casa?
2. ¿De qué color es tu cuarto?
3. El carro que quiere comprar Carlos es muy caro.

D. Dictado. You will hear a series of words. Each will be said twice. Listen carefully and write what you hear.

1. _____   3. _____   5. _____

2. _____   4. _____   6. _____

MINIDIÁLOGOS Y GRAMÁTICA

20. Expressing Negation: Indefinite and Negative Words

A. **¿Qué hay en el dibujo?** You will hear a series of sentences. Circle **C** if the sentence is true or **F** if it is false, according to the following drawing. First, stop the tape and look at the drawing.

1. C F   2. C F   3. C F   4. C F   5. C F

B. **Descripción.** You will hear a series of questions. Answer, according to the drawings.

MODELO: (*you hear*) ¿Hay algo en la pizarra? →
(*you say*) Sí, hay algo en la pizarra. Hay unas palabras.

1.

2.

3.

4.

5.

C. ¡Por eso no come nadie allí! You will hear a series of questions about a very unpopular restaurant. Each will be said twice. Answer, using the double negative.

> MODELO: (*you hear*) ¿Sirven algunos postres especiales? →
> (*you say*) No, no sirven ningún postre especial.

1. ... 2. ... 3. ... 4. ... 5. ...

D. Ningún cumpleaños es perfecto. Using some of the negative words you have learned and the oral cues, tell about your worst birthday.

> MODELOS: (*you hear*) cartas → (*you say*) No hay ninguna carta para mí.
>
> (*you hear*) bailar → (*you say*) Nadie quiere bailar conmigo.

1. ... 2. ... 3. ... 4. ... 5. ...

21. ¿Qué sabes y a quién conoces?: Saber and conocer; Personal a

A. Minidiálogo: Delante de un restaurante. You will hear a dialogue followed by a series of statements. Circle the number of the statement that best summarizes the main idea of the dialogue. In this exercise, you will practice listening for the main idea.

1. Amalia y Ernesto deciden almorzar en una cafetería.

2. Amalia y Ernesto deciden almorzar en casa de la tía de Ernesto.

3. Amalia y Ernesto deciden almorzar en el restaurante de la tía de Ernesto.

B. ¿Qué sabes y a quién conoces?

Paso 1. You will hear a brief paragraph about some of the things your friends know and whom they know. Listen and write either **sí** or **no** under the corresponding item. Two items have been done for you.

NOMBRE	BAILAR	JUAN	JUGAR AL TENIS	MIS PADRES	ESTA CIUDAD
Enrique	sí	no			
Roberto					
Susana					

Paso 2. Now answer the questions you hear with information from the completed chart. Check the answers to **Paso 1** in the Appendix before you begin **Paso 2.**

1. ... 2. ... 3. ... 4. ...

C. ¿De veras? (*Really?*) You have just made some statements to which your friend Armando reacts with surprise. Respond to his reaction, using **saber** or **conocer,** as appropriate.

> MODELO: (*you hear*) ¿Tú? ¿jugar al básquetbol? → (*you say*) Sí, sé jugar muy bien al básquetbol.

1. ... 2. ... 3. ... 4. ...

22. Expressing *What* or *Whom:* Direct Object Pronouns

A. Minidiálogo: ¿Dónde vamos a comer? You will hear a dialogue followed by two statements about the dialogue. Circle the number of the statement that best summarizes what happens in the dialogue. In this dialogue, you will practice listening for the main idea.

1. Mariela y Agustín tienen hambre y deciden invitar a sus amigos, los Velázquez, a cenar con ellos.

2. Mariela y Agustín tienen hambre y deciden cenar en el restaurante de los Velázquez.

B. Encuesta: ¿Qué te gusta comer? You will hear the names of various foods. Each will be said twice. Write in the blank the names of the food mentioned, then check the appropriate answer. No answers will be given on the tape. The answers you choose should be correct for you!

1. _____

   □ Siempre las como.

   □ Las como a veces.

   □ Nunca las como.

2. _____

   □ Siempre lo como.

   □ Lo como a veces.

   □ Nunca lo como.

3. _____

   □ Siempre la tomo.

   □ La tomo a veces.

   □ Nunca la tomo.

4. _____

   □ Siempre los como.

   □ Los como a veces.

   □ Nunca los como.

5. _____

   □ Siempre la como.

   □ La como a veces.

   □ Nunca la como.

C. En la cocina. You are preparing a meal, and your friend Pablo is in the kitchen helping you. Answer his questions, using object pronouns and the written cues. You will hear each question twice.

> MODELO: (*you hear*) ¿Necesitas la olla (*pan*) ahora?
> (*you see*) sí → (*you say*) ¿La olla? Sí, la necesito.
> (*you see*) no → (*you say*) ¿La olla? No, no la necesito todavía.

1. no 2. sí 3. sí 4. no 5. sí

D. Descripción: ¿Qué hacen estas personas? You will hear a series of questions. Answer, based on the drawings. Follow the model. First, stop the tape and look at the drawing.

MODELO: (*you hear*) ¿Un camarero toma el pedido (*order*)? → (*you say*) Sí, lo toma.

1. … 2. … 3. … 4. …

E. Entre amigos… Your friend Manuel, who hasn't seen you for a while, wants to know when you can get together again. Answer his questions, using the written cues. You will hear each question twice.

1. esta noche 2. para mañana 3. 4:00 4. Café La Rioja

F. Hablando de los estudios. You will hear a series of questions about why you haven't done certain things. Answer, using the written cues. Listen for the verb in each question.

MODELO: (*you hear*) ¿Por qué no *escribes* las cartas?
(*you see*) ya   → (*you say*) Ya las escribí.
           ir a   →   Voy a escribirlas.
           acabar de →   Acabo de escribirlas.

1. ya 2. ya 3. ir a 4. acabar de 5. acabar de

SITUACIONES

A. En un restaurante. In the following conversation you will hear an example of how to order from a menu. Read the conversation silently as you listen.

MANUEL: ¿Nos sentamos aquí?
ANAMARI: Perfecto. Aquí viene el camarero. ¿Por qué no pides tú la cena ya que conoces este restaurante?
CAMARERO: Buenas noches, señores. ¿Desean algo de aperitivo?
MANUEL: No, nada. Gracias. ¿Qué recomienda Ud. de comida?
CAMARERO: Los tacos «El Charro» son la especialidad de la casa. Como plato del día hay pez espada.
MANUEL: Bueno. De entrada, la sopa de tortillas. De plato fuerte, los tacos «El Charro». Ensalada de lechuga y tomate. Y de postre, flan. Para beber, agua mineral y, al final, dos cafés.

B. Now it's your turn to order. The same waiter will ask you questions about each part of the meal. Answer, based on the dialogue or based on your own preferences. You will hear a possible answer on the tape. The waiter will continue after you repeat the answer. First, stop the tape and read the menu.

❧ Restaurante el Charro ❧

Desayuno (de 8:00 a 11:00)   Precio fijo—

Frutas o jugo extra
Pan dulce o pan tostado (sweet rolls or toast)
Café   Té   Chocolate

Huevos rancheros (eggs with
    tomatoes, onions, and chiles) o
Huevos con jamón

Comida (de 1:00 a 4:00)   Precio fijo—

Antojitos (appetizers):
    Guacamole o cóctel de camarones
    (shrimp cocktail)
Sopas:
    Sopa de albóndigas (meatball soup) o
    Sopa de tortillas
Ensalada
Bebidas:
    Café   Té   Leche   Refrescos
    Agua mineral
    Cerveza o vino (blanco, tinto o
      rosado) extra

Platos fuertes (main courses):
- Tacos «El Charro» con salsa
   picante (hot sauce)
- Bistec con papas fritas
- Mole poblano de guajolote
   (turkey in a spicy sauce of chiles
   and chocolate)
- Pescado veracruzano (fish in a
   spicy sauce of tomatoes, chiles,
   onions, and green olives)

Tortillas o bolillos (rolls)
Postres: Helado, pastel de chocolate, flan

1. Favor de traerme...
2. Sí. Me trae... , por favor
3. ¿Todavía hay... ?
4. Entonces, me trae... , por favor
5. Quiero... , por favor
6. Favor de traerme...

UN POCO DE TODO (PARA ENTREGAR)

A. Descripción: La boda (*wedding*) **de Marisol y Gregorio.** You will hear a series of statements about the following drawing. Each will be said twice. Circle **C** if the statement is true or **F** if it is false. First, stop the tape and look at the drawing.

1. C F   2. C F   3. C F   4. C F   5. C F

B. *Listening Passage:* La vida social en los bares de España

Antes de escuchar. Before you listen to the passage, stop the tape and do the following prelistening exercises.

Many aspects of social life and nightlife in Spain are different from those of the United States. Check the ones that you think apply *only* to Spain.

□ Hay muchos bares. ¡A veces hay dos en cada calle!

□ La familia entera, padres e hijos pequeños, va al bar.

□ Por lo general, no se sirve comida.

□ Es costumbre pedir tapas: pequeños platos de comidas diversas.

Now turn on the tape.

Listening Passage. Now you will hear a passage about the many types of bars that are part of Spanish social life. The following words and phrases appear in the passage.

no tienen nada que ver con	*they have nothing to do with*
casero	*homemade, home-style*
el ambiente	*atmosphere*
sevillano	*de Sevilla*

Después de escuchar. Rewind the tape and listen to the passage again. Then stop the tape, and complete the following sentences with words chosen from the list.

Sevilla   amigos   tarde   tapas   café   frío   bar   Madrid

1. En España, los españoles van con frecuencia a un _____ o a un _____ para pasar el

   tiempo con los _____ y los compañeros.

2. En los bares, sirven _____, que son pequeños platos de comidas diversas.

3. Julia dice que prefiere la ciudad de _____ para divertirse. Allí no hace _____ en el

   invierno y la gente puede salir muy _____ todo el año.

Now turn on the tape.

C. Descripción: Un *picnic* en el parque. You will hear a series of questions. Each will be said twice. Answer, based on the drawing. Use direct object pronouns in your answers, when possible. Stop the tape and write the answers.

1. _____

2. _____

3. _____

4. _____

5. _____

D. En el periódico: Guía (*Guide*) de restaurantes. The following ads for restaurants appeared in a Spanish newspaper. Use them to answer the questions you will hear. Each question will be said twice. First, stop the tape and scan the ads. Stop the tape and write the answer.

1. _____
2. _____
3. _____
4. _____
5. _____

E. Y para terminar... Entrevista. You will hear a series of questions. Each will be said twice. Answer, based on your own experience. No answers will be given on the tape. Stop the tape and write the answer.

1. _____
2. _____
3. _____
4. _____
5. _____
6. _____

REPASO **2**

A. De compras con Sergio. You will hear a paragraph that describes a sequence of events. Listen carefully and number the drawings in the following series, from 1 to 5, according to the sequence of events described in the paragraph. One of the drawings does not belong at all. Cross it out. First, stop the tape and look at the drawings. In this exercise, you will practice listening for specific information, as well as putting events into the correct sequence.

a.

b.

c. _____

d.

e.

f.

B. Situaciones: Hablando de viajes. Imagine that you will travel to a variety of places this year. Answer the questions you hear about each of your trips, using the written cues. **¡OJO!** The questions may vary slightly from those seen in the model. Change your answers accordingly. You will hear a possible answer on the tape.

MODELO: (*you see*) March 30 / 2 / impermeable
(*you hear*) ¿Cuándo sales para Seattle? → (*you say*) Salgo el treinta de marzo.
(*you hear*) ¿Cuántas semanas vas a estar allí? → (*you say*) Creo que dos.
(*you hear*) ¿No llueve mucho en Seattle? → (*you say*) Sí. Por eso voy a llevar mi impermeable.

1. December 15 / 3 / traje de baño   3. September 1 / 2 / suéteres

2. February 29 / 1 / camisetas

C. Preguntas personales: Entrevista.

Paso 1. You write the gossip column for a newspaper and are assigned to interview a famous personality about his personal life, likes, dislikes, and so on. Formulate the questions you might ask him, using the written cues and an appropriate interrogative word. Add any other necessary words to complete the meaning of your question. You will hear an answer to your questions on the tape.

MODELO: (*you see*) ser / de → (*you say*) ¿De dónde es Ud.?   (*you hear*) Soy de Nueva York.

1. vivir (lugar)   4. ir (esta noche)

2. vivir con (persona)   5. llamarse (próxima película [*next movie*])

3. hacer (los fines de semana)

Paso 2. Now you will hear a series of statements about the answers that the famous personality gave. Each will be said twice. Circle **C** if the statement is true or **F** if it is false. If the information is not given, circle **ND** (**no lo dice**).

1. C F ND   3. C F ND   5. C F ND

2. C F ND   4. C F ND

D. En el restaurante La Valenciana. You are eating lunch, the main meal of the day, in a Spanish restaurant in Madrid. Use the menu below to answer the waiter's questions. You will hear a possible answer on the tape. First, listen to the items on the menu.

Entremeses:
Jamón serrano
Champiñones al ajillo (mushrooms sautéed in garlic)
Calamares fritos (fried squid)

Entradas:
Gazpacho andaluz (cold tomato soup served with condiments)
Ensalada mixta (mixed green salad)
Alcachofas salteadas con jamón (artichokes sautéed with ham)

Platos fuertes:
Solomillo a la parrilla (beef cooked over a grill)
Paella valenciana (rice dish with seafood, chicken, pork & saffron)
Cordero al chilindrón (lamb and red pepper stew)

Postres: *Bebidas:*
Flan de naranja (orange flan)   Jerez (sherry)   Vino tinto
Tarta de manzana (apple tart)   Té   Vino blanco
Peras al vino (pears in wine)   Café   Agua mineral

E. Hablando con el corredor de casas (*real-estate agent*) (**Para entregar**). You are a real-estate agent and your clients, Mr. and Mrs. Calvo, have some questions about a house that you are going to show them this afternoon. Each question will be said twice. Stop the tape and write your answers to their questions, based on the following floor plan. The following words appear in the questions or are useful for answering them. Listen to them before the questions are read.

mide	*it measures*
por	*by (e.g., 2 feet by 3 feet)*
el metro	*meter*

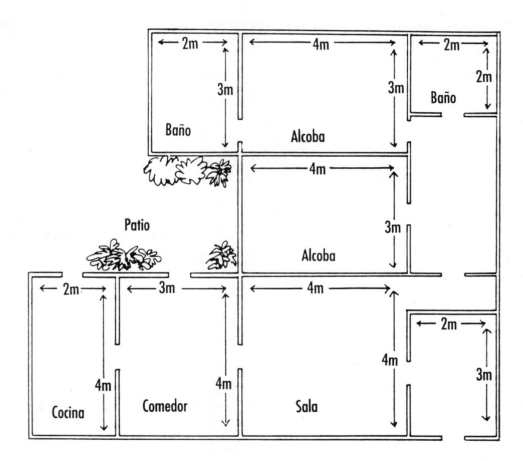

1. _____

2. _____

3. _____

4. _____

5. _____

F. Descripción (Para entregar). You will hear a series of questions. Each will be said twice. Base your answers on the following cartoon. Stop the tape and write the answers. The following words appear in the questions or are useful for answering them. Listen to them before the questions are read.

la taza   *cup*
veces   *times, occasions*
al final   *in the end*
por fin   *finally*

Now, stop the tape and look at the cartoon.

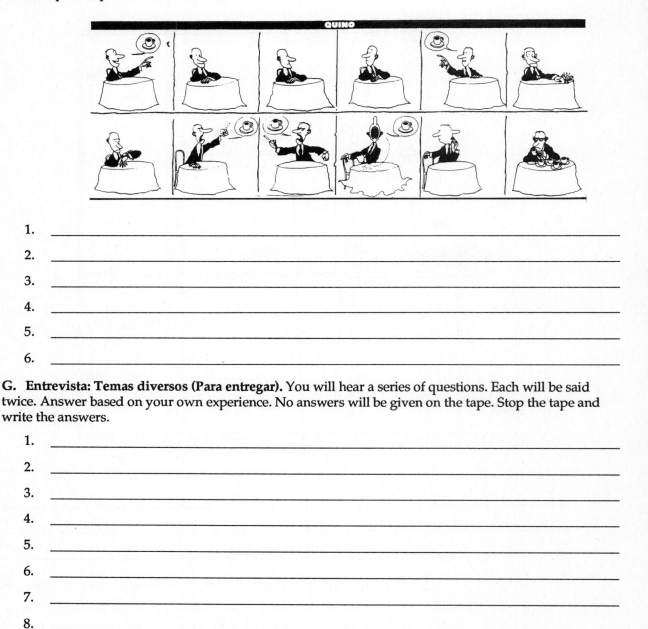

1. _____

2. _____

3. _____

4. _____

5. _____

6. _____

G. Entrevista: Temas diversos (Para entregar). You will hear a series of questions. Each will be said twice. Answer based on your own experience. No answers will be given on the tape. Stop the tape and write the answers.

1. _____

2. _____

3. _____

4. _____

5. _____

6. _____

7. _____

8. _____

9. _____

10. _____

CAPÍTULO **7**

VOCABULARIO: PREPARACIÓN

A. Encuesta: Hablando de sus últimas vacaciones. You will hear a series of statements about what you did on your last vacation. Indicate what is true for you by checking the appropriate answer. No answers will be given on the tape. The answers you choose should be correct for you!

1. □ Sí   □ No   3. □ Sí   □ No   5. □ Sí   □ No

2. □ Sí   □ No   4. □ Sí   □ No   6. □ Sí   □ No

B. Definiciones. You will hear a series of definitions. Each will be said twice. Circle the letter of the word that is best defined by each. **¡OJO!** There may be more than one answer in some cases.

1. a. el avión   b. la playa   c. el océano

2. a. el billete   b. la estación de trenes   c. el aeropuerto

3. a. el hotel   b. el restaurante   c. el maletero

4. a. el pasaje   b. la cabina   c. la salida

C. Situaciones: De viaje. You will hear a series of situations. Each will be said twice. Circle the letter of the best solution or response for each.

1. a. Salgo en dos semanas.

   b. Compro un boleto de ida y vuelta.

   c. Compro un boleto de ida.

2. a. ¡Estoy aburrido!

   b. ¡Estoy atrasado!

   c. ¡Estoy cansado!

3. a. Pido un pasaje de primera clase.

   b. Bajo del avión.

   c. Viajo en clase turística.

4. a. Pedimos asientos en la clase turística.

   b. Pedimos asientos en la sección de fumar.

   c. Pedimos asientos en la sección de no fumar.

5. a. Hago cola.

    b. Saco unas fotos.

    c. Facturo el equipaje.

D. Identificaciones. Identify the items after you hear the corresponding number. Begin each sentence with **Es…** or **Son…** and the appropriate indefinite article.

1. … 2. … 3. … 4. … 5. … 6. …

E. Hablando de viajes… Using the oral and written cues, tell your friend Benito, who has never traveled by plane, the steps he should follow to make an airplane trip.

MODELO: (*you see*) Primero… (*you hear*) llamar a la agencia de viajes →
(*you say*) Primero llamas a la agencia de viajes.

1. pedir
2. El día del viaje, …
3. facturar

4. Después…
5. Cuando anuncian la salida del vuelo, …
6. Por fin (*Finally*)…

F. ¿Dónde se hace… ? You will hear a series of statements about traveling. Each will be said twice. Circle **C** if the statement is true or **F** if it is false.

1. C F   2. C F   3. C F   4. C F

LOS HISPANOS HABLAN:
UNAS VACACIONES INOLVIDABLES

You will hear Cecilia's description of an unforgettable vacation. Then you will hear the following statements. Circle **C** if the statement is true or **F** if it is false. The following words appear in the description.

veranear	pasar el verano
partimos	*we left*
el colectivo	*type of taxi shared by several passengers*
hacernos cargo de	*take care of*
la aduana	*customs*
las valijas	las maletas
armamos la carpa	*we set up the tent*

1. C F Cecilia y su amiga pasaron (*spent*) el verano en las montañas.

2. C F Los padres de las muchachas pagaron (*paid for*) el viaje.

3. C F Cecilia y su amiga pasaron un mes en el Uruguay.

4. C F Había (*There were*) otra gente joven en la playa donde se quedaron (*stayed*) Cecilia y su amiga.

PRONUNCIACIÓN Y ORTOGRAFÍA: **P, T**

A. Like the [k] sound, Spanish **p** and **t** are not aspirated as they are in English. Compare the following pairs of aspirated and nonaspirated English sounds.

pin / spin   pan / span   tan / Stan   top / stop

Repeat the following words, phrases, and sentences, imitating the speaker.

1. pasar   padre   programa   puerta   esperar

2. tienda   todos   traje   estar   usted

3. una tía trabajadora   tres tristes tigres

   un tío tonto   pasar por la puerta

   unos pantalones pardos   un perro perezoso

4. Tomás toma tu té.   Papá paga el papel.

   También toma tu café.   Pero Pablo paga el periódico.

B. Repaso: p, t, k. You will hear a series of words. Each will be said twice. Circle the letter of the word you hear.

1. a. pata   b. bata   4. a. dos   b. tos

2. a. van   b. pan   5. a. de   b. té

3. a. coma   b. goma   6. a. callo   b. gallo

C. Dictado. You will hear four sentences. Each will be said twice. Listen carefully and write what you hear.

1. _____

2. _____

3. _____

4. _____

23. Expressing *to Whom* or *for Whom:* Indirect Object Pronouns; **dar** and **decir**

A. Mindiálogo: En la sala de espera del aeropuerto. You will hear a dialogue followed by a series of statements. Circle **C** if the statement is true or **F** if it is false. In this exercise, you will practice listening for specific information.

Sala de espera

1.   C   F   La madre y su hijo están en la estación del tren.

2.   C   F   La madre le compra otra revista a su hijo.

3.   C   F   El hijo acaba de comer y ahora quiere dulces.

4.   C   F   La madre no oye cuando anuncian el vuelo.

B.   Encuesta. You will hear a series of questions about your habits. Indicate what is true for you by checking the appropriate answer. No answers will be given on the tape. The answers you choose should be correct for you!

	SIEMPRE	A VECES	¡NUNCA!
1.	☐	☐	☐
2.	☐	☐	☐
3.	☐	☐	☐
4.	☐	☐	☐
5.	☐	☐	☐
6.	☐	☐	☐
7.	☐	☐	☐
8.	☐	☐	☐

C.   En casa durante la cena. Practice telling for whom the following things are being done, according to the model.

MODELO: *(you see)* Mi padre sirve el guacamole.   *(you hear)* a nosotros →
(you say) Mi padre *nos* sirve el guacamole.

1.   Mi madre sirve la sopa.

2.   Ahora ella prepara la ensalada.

3.   Mi hermano trae el café.

4.   Rosalinda da postre.

D. Descripción. Tell what the following people are doing, using the written cues with indirect object pronouns.

En la fiesta de aniversario de los Sres. Moreno

1. Susana: regalar   2. Miguel: mandar   3. Tito: regalar

En casa, durante el desayuno

4. Pedro: dar   5. Marta: dar   6. Luis: servir / todos

E. Preguntas. Practice telling about things we do for others and things others do for us. Each question will be said twice. Answer, using the written cues.

1. mi hermano menor
2. mi compañera de cuarto
3. mis amigos íntimos
4. mi novia
5. mis padres

24. Expressing Likes and Dislikes: **gustar**

A. Gustos y preferencias

Paso 1. You will hear a brief paragraph about some of the things some people like and dislike about traveling. Listen and write either **sí** or **no** under the corresponding item. Two items have been done for you.

NOMBRE	VIAJAR	LOS VUELOS LARGOS	HACER COLA	LAS DEMORAS
Enrique	sí	sí		
Roberto				
Susana				

Check the answers in the Appendix before you begin **Paso 2.**

Paso 2. Now answer the questions you hear with information from the completed chart.

    1. ...   2. ...   3. ...   4. ...

B. **¡Vamos de vacaciones! Pero... ¿adónde?** The members of the Soto family—of which you are one—can't decide where to go for their vacation. First, tell what each person likes, then tell where they should go, using the written cues.

    MODELOS: (*you see*) mi madre / esquiar → (*you say*) A mi madre le gusta esquiar.

                   (*you see*) ir a la playa → (*you say*) Le gustaría ir a la playa.

   1. mi hermana / esquiar; ir a Aspen

   2. mi padre / el arte italiano; viajar a Europa

   3. mis hermanitos / jugar afuera; visitar un parque nacional

   4. mí / la tranquilidad; quedarme en casa

C. **¿Qué le gusta? ¿Qué odia?** Using the written cues, tell what you like or hate about the following situations or locations. You will hear a possible answer on the tape.

    MODELO: (*you see and hear*) ¿En la universidad? (*you see*) fiestas / exámenes →
              (*you say*) Me gustan las fiestas. Odio los exámenes.

   1. ¿En la playa? nadar / sol   3. ¿En un parque? flores / insectos

   2. ¿En un restaurante? comida / música   4. ¿En un aeropuerto? viajar / demoras

D. Dictado: Una celebración

Paso 1. You will hear the following paragraphs. Listen carefully and write the missing words. Rewind the tape and listen again, if necessary.

Anita y Julio _____[1] ir a _____[2] fuera esta noche porque _____[3] el

cumpleaños de _____.[4] Anita hace reservaciones en el restaurante _____[5] que está

cerca de su apartamento _____[6] es el restaurante favorito de su _____.[7] A

_____[8] le _____[9] mucho la comida mexicana.

Cuando Anita y Julio _____ [10] al restaurante, el camarero _____ [11] enseña la

_____ [12] reservada, pero no _____ [13] gusta porque está _____ [14] cerca de

la _____. [15] Por fin encuentran una que _____ [16] _____ [17] situada y

_____ [18] piden el menú _____ [19] camarero. Después de _____, [20] Anita y

Julio _____ [21] indican al camarero lo que _____ [22] comer. Él _____ [23] trae

la comida y les dice «¡Buen provecho!». (*"Enjoy your meal!"*)

_____ [24] de cenar, Anita _____ [25] pide dos cafés y _____ [26] de

chocolate _____ [27] camarero. Él _____ [28] trae con la _____. [29]

Después de _____, [30] Anita le pregunta a Julio si le _____ [31] ir a bailar. Para

Julio, ¡fue un _____ [32] muy feliz!

Paso 2. Now you will hear a series of statements based on the preceding paragraphs. Each will be said twice. Circle **C** if the statement is true or **F** if it is false. If the information is not given, circle **ND** (**no lo dice**).

1. C F ND   3. C F ND   5. C F ND

2. C F ND   4. C F ND   6. C F ND

25. Influencing Others: Formal Commands

A. Minidiálogo: Un pasajero distraído. You will hear a dialogue followed by a series of statements about the dialogue. Circle **C** if the statement is true or **F** if it is false. If the information is not given, circle **ND** (**no lo dice**). In this exercise, you will practice listening for specific information.

1. C F ND   El pasajero tiene que usar el cinturón de seguridad.

2. C F ND   El pasajero toma asiento en la sección de fumar.

3. C F ND   El pasajero pierde su vuelo a Cuzco.

4. C F ND   La asistente no quiere ayudar al pasajero.

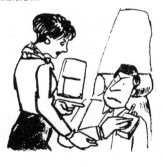

B. ¿Qué acaban de decir? You will hear a series of commands. Write the number of the command you hear next to the corresponding drawing. You will hear each statement twice. **¡OJO!** There is an extra drawing.

a. ___

b. ___

(Continúa.)

c. ___

d. ___

e. ___

C. Profesora por un día... You are the Spanish professor for the day. Practice telling your students what they should do, using the oral cues. Use **Uds.** commands.

1. ... 2. ... 3. ... 4. ... 5. ... 6. ...

D. La dieta del señor Casiano. Mr. Casiano is on a diet and you are his doctor. He will ask you whether or not he can eat certain things. Answer his questions, using affirmative or negative commands and direct object pronouns.

> MODELO: (*you hear*) ¿Puedo comer chocolate? (*you see*) No... →
> (*you say*) No, no lo coma.

1. No, ... 2. No, ... 3. No, ... 4. Sí, ... 5. Sí, ... 6. Sí, ...

E. Consejos para una persona desordenada. Mr. Larios is very careless about his appearance. Tell him to do the following things to improve his image.

> MODELO: (*you hear*) acostarse más temprano →
> (*you say*) Acuéstese más temprano.

1. ... 2. ... 3. ... 4. ... 5. ...

SITUACIONES

A. En la estación de autobuses. In the following conversation, you will hear one way to arrange for transportation. Read the conversation silently as you listen.

CLIENTE:	Por favor, un boleto para Guanajuato.
DEPENDIENTE:	Ya salió el último autobús con ese destino. Tiene que esperar hasta la tarde.
CLIENTE:	¿A qué hora sale el primero?
DEPENDIENTE:	Hay un autobús a las cuatro, otro a las cinco y media, otro a las siete, a las nueve y a las diez y cuarto.
CLIENTE:	Bien, déme un boleto para el de las cuatro. ¿Puedo sacar ahora el boleto de regreso para esta misma noche?
DEPENDIENTE:	Por supuesto. El último sale de Guanajuato a las diez.

B. Now you will participate in a similar conversation, partially printed in your manual, in which you arrange for transportation by train. Complete the conversation, using the written cues. Use the cues in the order given. First, listen to the cues.

1. Buenos días   2. de ida y vuelta   3. 1:00   4. 3:00

UD.: _____.[1] Me da un boleto _____[2] Panamá–Colón, por favor.

DEPENDIENTE: ¿Para qué tren? Hay uno a la una y otro a las tres.

UD.: Para el de _____.[3]

DEPENDIENTE: A ver… Lo siento, pero ya no hay asientos para ese tren.

UD.: Entonces, déme un boleto para el de _____.[4]

DEPENDIENTE: Aquí lo tiene. Son quince balboas. ¡Buen viaje!

UN POCO DE TODO (PARA ENTREGAR)

A. En el periódico: Anuncios. You will hear an ad for a Mexican airline company. It will be read twice. Then you will hear a series of statements. Circle **C** if the statement is true or **F** if it is false, based on the information contained in the ad and the following chart of departures. First, listen to the following phrases you will hear in the ad.

un viaje de negocios   *a business trip*
un viaje de placer   *a trip for pleasure*

MIAMI 10 vuelos semanales

	LUNES	MARTES	MIERCOLES	JUEVES	VIERNES	SABADO	DOMINGO
SALIDAS	11:50 Y 15:05	16:10	11:50 Y 16:10	15:15	11:50 Y 11:05	15:15	15:05

1. C F   2. C F   3. C F   4. C F

B. *Listening Passage:* **Un anuncio turístico**

Antes de escuchar. Stop the tape and do the following prelistening exercises.

Paso 1. Find out how much you know about Mexico's tourist attractions by answering the following questions. As you read the questions, try to infer the information the passage will give you, as well as the specific information for which you need to listen.

1. ¿Conoces México? ¿Sabes que la Ciudad de México es una de las ciudades más grandes del mundo, más grande aún que Nueva York? ¡Cuenta con 25.000.000 de habitantes!

2. ¿Sabes el nombre de algunos de los pueblos indígenas de México? Los olmecas y los toltecas son menos famosos que otros. ¿Cuáles son los más famosos?

Paso 2. Empareja (*Match*) el nombre de la ciudad mexicana con la atracción turística por la cual (*by which*) se conoce.

1. _____ la Ciudad de México
2. _____ Teotihuacán
3. _____ Acapulco
4. _____ Taxco
5. _____ Cancún

   a. ruinas mayas y playas bonitas
   b. objetos de plata (*silver*) y artesanías (*crafts*)
   c. las Pirámides del Sol y de la Luna
   d. playas
   e. el mejor museo antropológico del mundo

Now turn on the tape.

Listening Passage. Now, you will hear a travel ad about an excursion to Mexico. The following words appear in the passage.

Quinto centenario	quincentenary (500th anniversary)
el acercamiento	coming together
mezclar	to mix
la basílica	una iglesia grande
la plata	silver
relajarse	to relax
broncearse	to get a tan
el submarinismo	snorkeling
saborear	to taste
tentador	tempting
las plazas	spaces (on the tour)

Después de escuchar. Indicate the things that the tourists can do on this trip.

1. ☐ Pueden broncearse.

2. ☐ Hacen submarinismo.

3. ☐ Escalan (*They climb*) unas montañas muy altas.

4. ☐ Compran objetos de plata.

5. ☐ Pueden nadar en dos playas, por lo menos (*at least*).

6. ☐ Ven las ruinas de Machu Picchu.

7. ☐ Visitan un museo antropológico.

Now turn on the tape.

C. Entrevista: Hablando de vacaciones. You will hear a series of questions about your vacation plans. Each will be said twice. Answer, according to your own experience. No answers will be given on the tape. Stop the tape and write the answers.

1. _____

2. _____

3. _____

4. _____

D. Y para terminar… Descripción: En el avión. You will hear a series of questions. Each will be said twice. Answer, based on the drawing. First, stop the tape and look at the drawing. Then, as you hear the questions, stop the tape and write the answers.

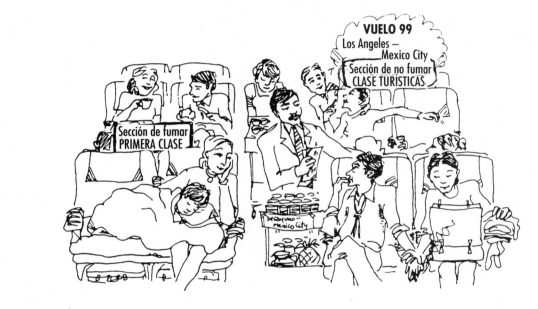

1. _____

2. _____

3. _____

4. _____

5. _____

6. _____

CAPÍTULO **8**

VOCABULARIO: PREPARACIÓN

A. Hablando de «cositas» (*"a few small things"*). You will hear a brief dialogue between two friends, Lidia and Daniel. Listen carefully and circle the items that are mentioned in their conversation. Don't be distracted by unfamiliar vocabulary. First, stop the tape and look at the drawing.

B. Definiciones. You will hear a series of statements. Each will be said twice. Circle the letter of the object that is defined by each.

1. a. la videocasetera   b. el Walkman

2. a. un descapotable   b. una camioneta

3. a. el cartel   b. el ratón

4. a. la jefa   b. el sueldo

5. a. la grabadora   b. el teléfono celular

6. a. el contestador automático   b. la motocicleta

7. a. el control remoto   b. la impresora

C. Identificaciones. Identify the following items when you hear the corresponding number. Begin each sentence with **Es una...** or **Es un...**

D. Hablando de lo que nos interesa. Your friends are telling you about the things that they have in their rooms. Based on what they say, try to guess what they enjoy. Choose interests from the following list. You will hear your friends' comments after you guess their interests. First, listen to the list.

la música   los deportes
el arte   las películas
los aparatos

MODELO: (*you hear*) En mi cuarto tengo muchos carteles de actores y actrices famosos. Tengo
           una videocasetera que uso constantemente. →
           (*you say*) Te interesan las películas, ¿verdad?   (*you hear*) Sí. ¡Me encantan!

1. ...   2. ...   3. ...   4. ...

LOS HISPANOS HABLAN: QUIERO...

Paso 1. Listen to Diana, José, and Karen describe what they want. As you listen to their descriptions, check the appropriate boxes. First, listen to the list of objects.

	DIANA	JOSÉ	KAREN
ropa	☐	☐	☐
un estéreo	☐	☐	☐
cosméticos	☐	☐	☐
cassettes	☐	☐	☐
discos	☐	☐	☐
una guitarra	☐	☐	☐
aretes (*earrings*)	☐	☐	☐
un auto	☐	☐	☐
un radio despertador	☐	☐	☐
un gran trabajo	☐	☐	☐

	DIANA	JOSÉ	KAREN
un boleto de avión	☐	☐	☐
una grabadora	☐	☐	☐
una batería (drum set)	☐	☐	☐
gafas oscuras	☐	☐	☐
una bicicleta	☐	☐	☐

Paso 2. Now you will hear a series of questions about the descriptions and the chart you completed in **Paso 1.** If you prefer, stop the tape and write the answers. Check your answers in the Appendix before you begin **Paso 2.**

1. _____

2. _____

3. _____

PRONUNCIACIÓN Y ORTOGRAFÍA: S, Z, CE, CI

A. The [s] sound in Spanish can be spelled several different ways and has several variants, depending on the country or region of origin of the speaker. Listen to the difference between these pronunciations of the [s] sound in two distinct Spanish-speaking areas of the world.[*]

Spain:	Vamos a llamar a Susana este lunes.
Latin America:	Vamos a llamar a Susana este lunes.
Spain:	Cecilia siempre cena con Alicia.
Latin America:	Cecilia siempre cena con Alicia.
Spain:	Zaragoza Zurbarán zapatería
Latin America:	Zaragoza Zurbarán zapatería

Notice also that in some parts of the Hispanic world, in rapid speech, the [s] sound becomes aspirated at the end of a syllable or word. Listen as the speaker pronounces these sentences.

¿Hasta cuándo vas a estar allí?   Les mandamos las cartas.

Allí están las mujeres.   Estos niños están sucios.

B. Repeat the following words and phrases, imitating the speaker.

1. sala   pastel   vaso   sopa   estantes   langostas

2. cien   cocina   piscina   ciudad   ciencias   cierto

3. arroz   actriz   azul   razón   perezoso   zapatos

4. estación   solución   situación   calefacción   acción

5. Siempre salgo a cenar con Zoila.   Los zapatos de Celia son azules.

   No conozco a Luz Mendoza de Pérez.   Esos discos están sucios.

---

[*] The Latin American variant of the [s] sound is used by most speakers in this tape program.

C. Repaso. You will hear a series of words spelled with **c** or **qu.** Each will be said twice. Circle the letter or letters used to spell each word.

1. c   qu   2. c   qu   3. c   qu   4. c   qu   5. c   qu   6. c   qu

MINIDIÁLOGOS Y GRAMÁTICA

26. Expressing Desires and Requests: Present Subjunctive: An Introduction; Use of the Subjunctive: Influence

A. Minidiálogo: Una compra importante. You will hear a dialogue followed by a series of statements. Circle **C** if the statement is true or **F** if it is false.

1. C   F   2. C   F   3. C   F   4. C   F

B. ¿Qué quiere Arturo?

Paso 1. You will hear Arturo talk about what he wants his siblings to do. Listen to what he says, and complete the following chart by checking the thing he wants each sibling to do or not to do.

PERSONA	NO JUGAR NINTENDO	NO USAR SU COCHE	PRESTARLE SU CÁMARA	BAJAR EL VOLUMEN DEL ESTÉREO
su hermana				
su hermano menor				
sus hermanitos				

Paso 2. Now answer the questions you hear, based on the completed chart. Each question will be said twice. Check the answers in the Appendix before you begin **Paso 2.**

1. ...   2. ...   3. ...   4. ...

C. Antes del viaje: ¿Qué quiere Ud. que hagan estas personas? You are a tour leader, traveling with a large group of students. Using the oral and written cues, tell each person what you want him or her to do. Begin each sentence with **Quiero que...** , as in the model.

MODELO: (*you hear*) hacer las maletas   (*you see*) Uds. →
(*you say*) Quiero que Uds. hagan las maletas.

1. Toño   2. (tú)   3. Ana y Teresa   4. todos   5. todos   6. todos

D. ¿Qué recomienda el nuevo jefe? You have a new boss in your office, and he is determined to make some changes. Tell what he recommends, using the written cues.

MODELO: (*you see*) El jefe recomienda... Ud. / buscar otro trabajo →
(*you say*) El jefe recomienda que Ud. busque otro trabajo.

1. El jefe recomienda... yo / no llegar tarde

2. El jefe insiste... todos / trabajar hasta muy tarde

3. El jefe prohíbe... Federico / dormir en la oficina

4. El jefe pide... (nosotros) / ser puntuales

5. El jefe prohíbe... tú / fumar en la oficina

E. Dictado: De vacaciones. You will hear a series of sentences. Each will be said twice. Listen carefully and write the missing words.

1. El inspector _____ que los turistas _____ _____ los pasaportes.

2. Paquita y yo _____ que _____ con nosotros.

3. El señor Hurtado _____ que su esposa _____ al tenis.

4. Antonio _____ que _____ por barco.

5. La asistente _____ que _____ mientras despegamos.

6. _____ _____ que todos _____ temprano al aeropuerto.

27. Expressing Feelings: Use of the Subjunctive: Emotion

A. Minidiálogo: Las desventajas de la tecnología. You will hear a dialogue followed by a series of statements. Circle the letter of the person who might have made each statement.

a = Marisa   b = Carlos

1. a b Normalmente no estás en casa a estas horas.

2. a b Perdí todo mi trabajo cuando me falló la computadora.

3. a b Deben comprarte una nueva computadora.

4. a b Por fin estoy en casa durante el día y... ¡no puedo mirar la tele porque no funciona!

B. ¿Qué sientes? Practice telling how you feel about the following things, using the oral cues. Add any necessary words.

MODELO: (you see) no venir nadie / a mi fiesta   (you hear) tener miedo de que →
(you say) Tengo miedo de que no venga nadie a mi fiesta.

1. mis padres / estar bien

2. mi auto / no funcionar

3. los vecinos / poner el estéreo a las dos de la mañana

4. mis amigos / llamarme con frecuencia

5. (tú) / no tener trabajo

C. Descripción: Esperanzas (*Hopes*) **y temores** (*fears*). You will hear two questions about each drawing. Answer, based on the drawings and the written cues.

1. sacar (*to get*) malas notas (*grades*) / sacar una «A»
2. funcionar su computadora / fallarle la computadora
3. haber regalos para él / no haber nada para él

D. Comentarios sobre la vida universitaria. Your friend Nuria will make a series of statements (printed in your manual). React to her statements, using the oral cues.

> MODELO: (*you see and hear*) El profesor nos da otro examen. (*you hear*) me sorprende →
> (*you say*) Me sorprende que el profesor nos **dé** otro examen.

1. El profesor no está en clase hoy.
2. La bibliotecaria pierde los libros.
3. Los estudiantes no vienen a clase los viernes.
4. No dormimos en clase.
5. No practicas un deporte.
6. No tenemos clases mañana.

28. Expressing Direct and Indirect Objects Together: Double Object Pronouns

A. En casa, durante la cena. During dinner, your brother asks about the different foods that might be left. He will say each question twice. Listen carefully and circle the items to which he is referring.

> MODELO: (*you hear*) ¿Hay más? Me la pasas, por favor. →
>
> (*you see*) (la sopa) el pan el pescado

1. las galletas   la fruta   el helado
2. la carne   el postre   los camarones
3. la leche   el vino   las arvejas
4. las papas fritas   la cerveza   el pastel

B. ¿Dónde está? Carolina would like to borrow some things from you. Tell her to whom you gave each item, basing your answer on the written cues and selecting the correct pronouns. You will hear each of Carolina's questions twice. *Note:* **presté** means *I lent*.

> MODELO: (*you hear*) Oye, ¿dónde está tu diccionario?
> (*you see*) Se (lo/la) presté a Nicolás. Él (lo/la) necesita para un examen. →
> (*you say*) Se lo presté a Nicolás. Él lo necesita para un examen.

1. Se (lo/la) presté a Nicolás. Él (lo/la) necesita para un viaje.

2. Se (los/las) presté a Teresa. Ella (los/las) necesita para su fiesta.

3. Se (la/las) presté a Juan. Él (la/las) necesita para escribir un trabajo.

4. Se (lo/la) presté a Nina. Ella (lo/la) necesita para ir al parque.

C. En el Restaurante El Charro. You will hear a series of questions. Each will be said twice. Answer, based on the drawings, and use double object pronouns in your answers. The correct verb form is provided for you in each case.

1. da   2. sirve   3. sirve   4. pasa

SITUACIONES

A. En una tienda de computadoras. In the following dialogue, you will hear one way to ask for service in a store. Read the dialogue silently as you listen.

DEPENDIENTE: Buenas. ¿Qué desea?
CLIENTE: Necesito que me arreglen esta impresora.
DEPENDIENTE: Puede dejarla. Alguien la va a ver mañana o pasado mañana.
CLIENTE: Pero… tengo un trabajo importante que hacer y quisiera tenerla pronto.
DEPENDIENTE: ¿La compró Ud. aquí?
CLIENTE: Sí, aquí tiene el recibo y la garantía.
DEPENDIENTE: Bueno, llévela allí delante. Alguien la va a atender en seguida.
CLIENTE: Muchas gracias.

B. Now you will participate in a similar conversation, partially printed in your manual. Use expressions from the following list to complete the conversation. The expressions are in the correct order. First, listen to the list of expressions.

1. Buenos días
2. monitor
3. escribir un informe importantísimo
4. me lo arreglen esta tarde
5. Mil gracias

DEPENDIENTE: Buenos días. ¿En qué puedo servirle?

UD.: _____.1

Este _____2 no funciona y quiero que me lo arreglen.

DEPENDIENTE: No hay problema. Si no es algo serio, puede recogerlo en dos o tres días. Si es algo complicado, es posible que tardemos una semana o más en arreglarlo.

UD.: El problema es que tengo que _____.3

Necesito que _____.4

DEPENDIENTE: Bueno, si se trata de un caso de urgencia, se lo arreglamos inmediatamente.

UD.: _____.5

UN POCO DE TODO (PARA ENTREGAR)

A. Diálogo: En la tienda de computadoras. You will hear a conversation followed by a series of statements. Circle **C** if the statement is true or **F** if it is false. The following words appear in the conversation.

principiantes	beginners
aplicaciones	applications, uses
reparar	to repair
hojas	sheets (of paper)

1. C F   2. C F   3. C F   4. C F   5. C F

B. Descripción: Una familia de la era de la tecnología. You will hear five brief descriptions. Write the letter of each description next to the drawing that it describes. ¡OJO! Not all the drawings will be described. First, stop the tape and look at the drawings.

1. ___

2. ___

3. ___

4. ___

5. __    6. __

C. *Listening Passage:* **Recuerdos de España**

Antes de escuchar. Stop the tape and do the following prelistening exercise.

Answer these questions about Spain to see how much you already know about this European country.

1. ¿Cómo piensas que es el nivel de vida (*standard of living*) en España?

2. ¿Crees que España ha cambiado (*has changed*) mucho en los últimos treinta años?

3. ¿Sabes lo que es la Comunidad Europa (la CE)? España pertenece (*belongs*) a ella desde 1986.

4. ¿Cuántas semanas de vacaciones te dan al año si trabajas en los Estados Unidos? ¿Y en España?

Now turn on the tape.

Listening Passage. Now you will hear a passage in which a person from Spain tells us about his homeland. The following words appear in the passage.

a finales de	*at the end of*
en vías de desarrollo	*developing*
a nivel	*at the level*
las cuestiones	*matters*
incluso	*even*
occidental	*western*
con eficacia	*efficiently*
los medios	*means*
el ascenso	*promotion*
Me he americanizado.	*I have become Americanized.*

Después de escuchar

Paso 1. You will hear a series of incomplete statements. Each will be said twice. Circle the letter of the word or phrase that best completes each.

1. a. joven

    b. de mediana edad

    c. viejo

2. a. en España

    b. en los Estados Unidos

    c. en Latinoamérica

3. a. visiten España, pero que estudien en los Estados Unidos

    b. vivan en España permanentemente

    c. vivan en los Estados Unidos y estudien en España.

Paso 2. Listen to the passage again. Then, stop the tape and check all the statements that, according to speaker of the passage, describe present-day Spain.

1. □ España es un país en vías de desarrollo.

2. □ El nivel de vida en las ciudades grandes es bueno.

3. □ A los españoles no les gusta trabajar.

4. □ Es normal que los españoles tengan cuatro semanas de vacaciones al año.

5. □ Las universidades españolas tienen un mejor sistema de bibliotecas que las estadounidenses.

6. □ España es un país moderno y desarrollado (*developed*).

7. □ La Comunidad Europea ha beneficiado (*has benefitted*) a España.

Now turn on the tape.

D. En el periódico: Clasificados. The following ads appeared in Hispanic newspapers. Decide which item you would most like to purchase, and answer the questions. If the ad for the item you wish to purchase does not have the information asked for in the questions, write **No lo dice.** No answers will be given on the tape. Stop the tape and write the answers. First, stop the tape and look at the ad for the item you want to buy.

1. _____

2. _____

3. _____

4. _____

5. _____

E. Y para terminar… Entrevista. You will hear a series of questions. Each will be said twice. Answer, based on your own experience. No answers will be given on the tape. Stop the tape and write the answers.

1. _____

2. _____

3. _____

4. _____

5. _____

6. _____

CAPÍTULO **9**

VOCABULARIO: PREPARACIÓN

A. Gustos y preferencias. You will hear a series of descriptions of what people like to do. Each will be said twice. Listen carefully, and circle the letter of the activity or activities that are best suited to each person.

1. a. nadar   b. jugar al ajedrez   c. tomar el sol

2. a. dar fiestas   b. ir al teatro   c. ir a un bar

3. a. ir a un museo   b. hacer *camping*   c. hacer un *picnic*

4. a. patinar   b. esquiar   c. correr

5. a. correr   b. ir a un museo   c. ir al cine

B. Encuesta: ¿Con qué frecuencia haces estos quehaceres? You will hear a series of questions about your habits. For each question, check the appropriate answer. No answers will be given on the tape. The answers you choose should be correct for you!

	SIEMPRE	A VECES	¡NUNCA!
1.	☐	☐	☐
2.	☐	☐	☐
3.	☐	☐	☐
4.	☐	☐	☐
5.	☐	☐	☐
6.	☐	☐	☐
7.	☐	☐	☐
8.	☐	☐	☐

C. Descripción: El apartamento de David y Raúl. You will hear a series of statements about the following drawing. Each will be said twice. Circle **C** if the statement is true or **F** if it is false. First, stop the tape and look at the drawing.

1. C F   2. C F   3. C F   4. C F   5. C F

D. Anuncios: Se venden aparatos domésticos. You will hear a series of ads for appliances. Each will be said twice. Write the number of the ad next to the appliance described. First, listen to the list of appliances.

___ una estufa   ___ un refrigerador

___ una secadora   ___ un aire acondicionador

E. ¿Para qué sirven estos aparatos domésticos? Your young friend Joselito wants to know what various appliances do. Answer his questions, using phrases chosen from the following list. You will hear each of his questions twice. First, listen to the list. **¡OJO!** Not all the expressions will be used.

tostar (ue) el pan   lavar los platos sucios
congelar la carne y las verduras   secar la ropa mojada (*wet*)
acondicionar el aire   cocinar la comida rápidamente
lavar la ropa sucia   hacer el café

MODELO: (*you hear*) ¿Para qué sirve la cafetera? → (*you say*) Hace el café.

1. ...   2. ...   3. ...   4. ...   5. ...

F. ¿Qué quieres que hagan estas personas? It's Saturday morning, and you want the whole family to help with the chores. Tell each member of your imaginary family what to do, using the oral and written cues. **¡OJO!** You will be using the subjunctive in the dependent clause.

MODELO: (*you see*) todos   (*you hear*) limpiar la casa →
          (*you say*) Quiero que todos limpien la casa.

1. Juana y Ceci   2. (tú)   3. Antonio   4. mi esposo   5. todos

LOS HISPANOS HABLAN:
¿CUÁL ES TU PASATIEMPO FAVORITO?

Paso 1. You will hear two answers to this question. Listen carefully and jot down notes about what each person says. The following words appear in the answers.

los aparadores	*display windows*
las sodas	*soda fountains*
los bancos	*benches*
la natación	*swimming*

Xiomara:

_____

_____

_____

_____

Gabriela:

_____

_____

_____

_____

Paso 2. Now, stop the tape and answer these questions.

1. ¿Qué actividades tienen en común las dos jóvenes?

_____

2. ¿Qué pasatiempos no tienen en común Gabriela y Xiomara?

_____

Now turn on the tape.

PRONUNCIACIÓN Y ORTOGRAFÍA: **J, G, GU**

A. The [x] sound can be written as **j** (before all vowels), or as **g**, before **e** and **i**. Its pronunciation varies, depending on the region or country of origin of the speaker. Note the difference in the pronunciation of these words.

España:	Jorge	jueves	gente	álgebra
el Caribe:	Jorge	jueves	gente	álgebra

B. Repeat the following words and phrases, imitating the speaker.

1. Jalisco   jirafa   fijo   extranjero   mujer   joven   viejo   consejera

2. general   generoso   inteligente   geografía   región   religión   sicología   biología

3. una región geográfica   una mujer generosa   un consejero joven

C. The [g] sound is written as **g** before the vowels **a, o,** and **u,** and as **gu** before **e** and **i.** In addition, it has two variants. At the beginning of a word, after a pause, or after **n,** it is pronounced like the *g* in *get.* In all other positions, it has a softer sound produced by allowing some air to escape when it is pronounced. There is no exact equivalent for this second variant in English.

Repeat the following words and sentences, imitating the speaker.

1. [g] grande   tengo   gusto   gracias   guapo   ganga

2. [g̵] amiga   diálogo   pagar   regatear   delgado   el gorila

3. Tengo algunas amigas guatemaltecas.   ¿Cuánto pagaste?

   ¡Qué ganga!   Domingo es guapo y delgado.

D. Dictado. You will hear five sentences. Each will be said twice. Listen carefully and write what you hear.

1. _____

2. _____

3. _____

4. _____

5. _____

MINIDIÁLOGOS Y GRAMÁTICA

29. Talking About the Past (2): Preterite of Regular Verbs and of *dar, ir,* and *ser*

A. Minidiálogo: Un problema con un compañero de casa. You will hear a dialogue followed by a series of statements. Circle the letter of the person who might have made each statement.

Compañeros de casa: a = Ceci, b = Julio. Una amiga: c = Graciela.

1. a   b   c   No hice nada ayer.

2. a   b   c   Mis amigos me visitaron ayer.

3. a   b   c   Julio es mejor que tu otro compañero de casa.

4. a   b   c   ¡Mi compañero de casa es un desastre!

5. a   b   c   Estoy de vacaciones.

B. Encuesta: Hablando de lo que hiciste ayer. You will hear a series of statements about what you did yesterday. For each statement, check the appropriate answer. No answers will be given on the tape. The answers you choose should be correct for you!

1. □ Sí   □ No   5. □ Sí   □ No

2. □ Sí   □ No   6. □ Sí   □ No

3. □ Sí   □ No   7. □ Sí   □ No

4. □ Sí   □ No   8. □ Sí   □ No

C. ¿Presente o pretérito? You will hear a series of brief conversations or parts of conversations. Listen carefully, and determine if the people are talking about the past or the present. Don't be distracted by unfamiliar vocabulary.

1. a. presente   b. pretérito   4. a. presente   b. pretérito
2. a. presente   b. pretérito   5. a. presente   b. pretérito
3. a. presente   b. pretérito

D. ¿Qué hizo Nadia anoche? You will hear a series of statements. Each will be said twice. Write the number of each statement next to the drawing that is described by that statement. First, stop the tape and look at the drawings. Nadia's friend is Guadalupe.

E. ¿Qué pasó ayer? Practice telling what the following people did yesterday, using the oral and written cues.

Antes de la fiesta

1. (yo)
2. mi compañero
3. (nosotros)

Antes del examen de química

4. Nati y yo
5. Diana
6. todos

El verano pasado

7. (tú)
8. (yo)
9. los niños

F. El viaje de los Sres. Blanco. You will hear a series of questions about Mr. and Ms. Blanco's recent plane trip to Lima, Peru. Answer, using the written cues.

1. 10:10 A.M.
2. el Sr. Ortega
3. leer revistas

4. 11:00 P.M.
5. el hotel

30. ¿Qué estás haciendo?: Present Progressive: estar + -ndo

A. ¿Qué están haciendo? You will hear a series of sentences. Each will be said twice. Write the number of each statement next to the item that corresponds to the activity mentioned. First, listen to the list of items.

a. ___ el menú

b. ___ las bicicletas

c. ___ el libro

d. ___ la computadora

e. ___ la música

f. ___ los zapatos de tenis

B. Descripción: ¿Qué están haciendo en este momento? Using the present progressive of the following verbs, tell what each person in the Hernández family is doing at the moment. Don't attach the reflexive pronouns to the present participle. First, listen to the list of verbs.

ponerse afeitarse jugar vestirse dormir bañarse

MODELO: (*you hear*) 1. ... → (*you say*) El bebé está durmiendo.

2. ...   3. ...   4. ...   5. ...   6. ...

C. Un fin de semana típico. Your family doesn't help much with the household chores. Nobody did anything last week, and now you are doing it all on the weekend. Tell what you are doing at this moment, using the oral cues. Attach the object pronouns to the present participle. Follow the model.

     MODELO: (*you hear*) Nadie lavó los platos. → (*you say*) Por eso estoy lavándo**los** ahora.

1. ... 2. ... 3. ... 4. ... 5. ...

31. Expressing *Each Other:* Reciprocal Actions with Reflexive Pronouns

Descripción: ¿Qué hacen estas personas? Using the written cues, tell what the following pairs of people are doing when you hear the corresponding number. You will be describing reciprocal actions. You will hear a possible answer on the tape.

1. quererse mucho
2. escribirse con frecuencia

3. darse la mano (*to shake hands*)
4. hablarse por teléfono

SITUACIONES

A. Un fin de semana con los parientes. You will hear a conversation about how Hildebrando spent his weekend. Read the dialogue silently as you listen.

HILDEBRANDO: ¿Qué tal el fin de semana?
MARIPEPA: Tranquilo como siempre. ¿Y tú? ¿Fuiste a algún sitio?
HILDEBRANDO: Pasé el fin de semana en casa de mis padres. Nos juntamos los cinco hermanos. Mi hermana Elisa fue a recoger a mis abuelos y yo me quedé con mi padre trabajando en el jardín.
MARIPEPA: Bueno, pero seguro que no te pasaste todo el tiempo trabajando.
HILDEBRANDO: ¡Claro que no! Me levanté tarde. Luego comimos, vimos la tele, jugamos al básquetbol, hicimos galletas… Vamos, un fin de semana muy típico.

B. Now you will participate in a similar conversation, partially printed in your manual, about what you do on the weekend. Complete it, using the written cues in the order given. First, listen to the cues.

1. ir de compras

2. hacer la limpieza (*cleaning*)

3. cuándo / hacer (tú) / los quehaceres

SU AMIGA: ¿Qué haces los fines de semana?

UD.: Normalmente, _____ [1] o

_____ .[2]

¿Y tú?

SU AMIGA: Pues a mí me gusta pasear en bicicleta, si hace buen tiempo, claro. Si llueve, me gusta

alquilar una película.

UD.: Y ¿ _____ [3]?

SU AMIGA: ¿Los quehaceres? Ah,... Es que los hace mi compañero de casa. ¡A mí sólo me toca

cocinar!

UN POCO DE TODO (PARA ENTREGAR)

A. Descripción: En casa de los Delibes. You will hear a series of statements about the following drawing. Each will be said twice. Circle **C** if the statement is true or **F** if it is false. First, stop the tape and look at the drawing.

1. C F   2. C F   3. C F   4. C F   5. C F   6. C F

B. *Listening Passage: ¿Cómo se pasan los fines de semana y los días de fiesta?*

Antes de escuchar. *Stop the tape* and do the following prelistening exercise.

Before you listen to the passage, read the following statements about how some people spend weekends or holidays. Check those statements that are true for you and your family.

☐ Los fines de semana son ocasiones familiares.

☐ Pasamos los fines de semana o los días de fiesta en nuestra casa en el campo.

☐ Mi madre siempre prepara una comida especial los domingos.

□ Paso el fin de semana con mis amigos y no con mi familia.

□ Después de comer, toda la familia sale a dar un paseo por el parque.

□ Paso el fin de semana con mis abuelos.

Now turn on the tape.

Listening Passage. Now you will hear a passage about how some Hispanics spend their weekends and holidays. The following words appear in the passage.

adinerados	*well-to-do*
a mediodía	*at noon*
el hogar	*home*
el descanso	*rest*
se suele	*it is the custom (to)*
elegir	*to choose, pick*
los columpios	*swings*
los críos	*young children*
charlando	*chatting, talking*
relajados	*relaxed*

Después de escuchar. Now you will hear a series of statements. Each will be said twice. Circle **C** if the statement is true or **F** if it is false. Stop the tape and correct the statements that are false, according to the passage.

1. C F _____

2. C F _____

3. C F _____

4. C F _____

5. C F _____

Now turn on the tape.

C. Y para terminar… Entrevista: Hábitos y costumbres. You will hear a series of questions. Each will be said twice. Answer, based on your own experience. No answers will be given on the tape. Stop the tape and write the answers.

1. _____

2. _____

3. _____

4. _____

5. _____

6. _____

7. _____

8. _____

REPASO 3

A. You will hear five brief conversations or parts of conversations. Write the number of each conversation in the appropriate blank to indicate where it might have taken place. First, listen to the locations.

___ un restaurante   ___ una oficina

___ un avión   ___ la sala de espera de un aeropuerto

___ la estación del tren

B. Anuncios. You will hear three brief travel ads. Write the number of the ad next to the person or persons who might like the vacation described. First, listen to the description of the persons who are planning their vacations.

____ *Felipe* es un estudiante y nunca ha viajado a un país extranjero. Para sus vacaciones quiere viajar lejos de su casa, pero no tiene mucho dinero.

____ *Los Sres. Brown* viven en Alaska y piensan ir de vacaciones en enero porque odian el clima de Alaska durante el invierno.

____ *Anita y Luisa* son muy deportistas (*sports-minded*) y cada vez que van de vacaciones les gusta ir a lugares que ofrezcan la oportunidad de practicar actividades deportivas.

C. ¿Qué quieren Uds. que hagan estas personas? Using the following list of phrases, answer the questions you hear on tape. You will be telling what you want a series of people to do for you and a friend. You will hear each question twice. First, listen to the list.

servirnos la comida   llamar a la doctora
darnos un aumento (*raise*)   arreglar la computadora
no poner la radio a las 11:00 P.M.

MODELO: ¿Qué quieren Uds. que haga el enfermero (*nurse*)? →
Queremos que llame a la doctora.

1. ...   2. ...   3. ...   4. ...

D. Preguntas: ¿Qué pasó hoy? You will hear a series of questions. Each will be said twice. Answer, using the written cues.

1. levantarse / bañarse

2. preparar el desayuno / leer el periódico

3. lavar los platos / llevar la basura al garaje

4. hablar (yo) con unos amigos / invitarlos (yo) a una fiesta

5. mirar la televisión / acostarse a las once

E. Descripción: En casa de la familia Ruiz. You will hear a series of statements about the following drawing. Circle **C** if the statement is true or **F** if it is false. Then you will be asked to describe some of the actions in the drawing. First, stop the tape and look at the drawing.

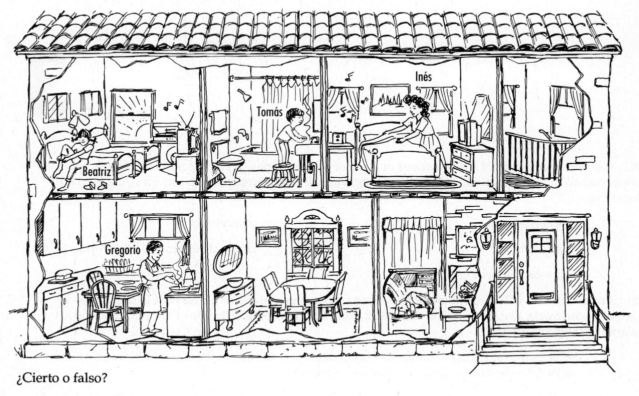

¿Cierto o falso?

1. C F   2. C F   3. C F   4. C F

Descripción

1. …   2. …   3. …   4. …

F. En el periódico: Se venden computadoras. Stop the tape and look at the ad on the next page. When you hear the numbers, give the Spanish equivalent of the English words. Then, you will hear some questions about the ad.

1. hard disc 2. monochrome 3. tutorials 4. regulator 5. ... 6. ... 7. Era (*It was*) válido...

G. Dictado (Para entregar). You will hear a conversation between a tourist who is interested in traveling to Cancún and a travel agent. Listen carefully and write down the requested information. First, listen to the list of information that is being requested.

el tipo de boleto que el turista quiere: _____

la fecha de salida: _____

la fecha de regreso (*return*): _____

la sección y la clase en que va a viajar: _____

la ciudad de la cual (*from which*) va a salir el avión: _____

el tipo de hotel que quiere: _____

el nombre del hotel en que se va a quedar: _____

H. Entrevista: Temas diversos (Para entregar). You will hear a series of questions. Each will be said twice. Answer based on your own experience, using direct and indirect object pronouns whenever possible. No answers will be given on the tape. Stop the tape and write the answers.

1. _____

2. _____

3. _____

4. _____

5. _____

6. _____

7. _____

CAPÍTULO **10**

VOCABULARIO: PREPARACIÓN

A. **¿Una fiesta familiar típica?** You will hear a description of Sara's last family gathering. Then you will hear a series of statements. Circle **C** if the statement is true or **F** if it is false. If the information is not given, circle **ND** (**no lo dice**).

1. C F ND Según lo que dice Sara, sus fiestas familiares normalmente son muy divertidas.

2. C F ND A la tía Eustacia le gusta discutir con el padre de Sara.

3. C F ND Normalmente, los primos de Sara se portan mal en las fiestas familiares.

4. C F ND Sara no se lleva bien con su familia.

5. C F ND Los hermanos de Sara discuten mucho con sus padres.

B. **Días festivos.** You will hear a series of dates. Each will be said twice. Circle the letter of the holiday that is usually celebrated on that date.

1. a. la Noche Vieja   b. la Nochebuena

2. a. el Día de los Muertos   b. el Día del Año Nuevo

3. a. la Navidad   b. la Pascua

4. a. el Día de los Muertos   b. la Noche Vieja

5. a. la Pascua Florida   b. el Día de Gracias

C. **¿Cómo reacciona Ud.?** Practice telling how you react to these situations, using the oral and written cues. Use the word **cuando** in each sentence.

MODELO: (*you see*) Me olvido del cumpleaños de mi madre. (*you hear*) ponerme avergonzado →
(*you say*) Me pongo avergonzada cuando me olvido del cumpleaños de mi madre.

1. Mi novio se enoja conmigo.   4. Hablo con mis profesores.

2. Mis padres me quitan el coche.   5. Saco buenas notas (*grades*).

3. Veo una película triste.

D. El mejor restaurante del mundo. You will hear a series of questions about the "world's best restaurant." Each will be said twice. Answer, using an emphatic form of the indicated adjective or adverb.

MODELO: *(you hear)* ¿Qué tal la ensalada? *(you see)* sabroso *(tasty)* → *(you say)* Es sabrosísima.

1. rico 2. bueno 3. caro 4. rápido

E. Descripción: Una fiesta de la Noche Vieja. Describe how these people feel or what they are doing, by answering the questions you hear. Each will be said twice.

1. ... 2. ... 3. ... 4. ... 5. ... 6. ...

LOS HISPANOS HABLAN: UNA FIESTA INOLVIDABLE

You will hear Karen and Xiomara talk about two unforgettable parties. The following words appear in the descriptions.

las damas	*ladies (maids of honor)*	orgulloso	*proud*
el vals	*waltz*	el brindis	*toast*
duró	*lasted*	he pasado	*I have spent*
estuvo presente	*were there*		

Now, stop the tape and indicate the statements that can be inferred from the information given in the two descriptions.

1. □ La quinceañera (fiesta de los quince años) es una fiesta importante para Karen y Xiomara.

2. □ Hay muchos invitados en estas fiestas.

3. □ La quinceañera es una fiesta que dura *(lasts)* hasta muy tarde.

4. □ Karen y Xiomara celebraron su quinceañera en los Estados Unidos.

5. □ En estas fiestas hay música.

Now turn on the tape.

PRONUNCIACIÓN Y ORTOGRAFÍA: Ñ, CH

A. The pronunciation of the letter ñ is similar to the sound [ny] in the English words *canyon* and *union*. However, in Spanish it is pronounced as one single sound.

Repeat the following words and sentences, imitating the speaker.

1. cana / caña   sonar / soñar   mono / moño   tino / tiño   cena / seña

2. año   señora   cañón   español   pequeña   compañero

3. El señor Muñoz es de España.

   Los niños pequeños no enseñan español.

   La señorita Ordóñez tiene veinte años.

   El cumpleaños de la señora Yáñez es mañana.

B. You will hear a series of words. Each will be said twice. Circle the letter of the word you hear.

1. a. pena   b. peña

2. a. una   b. uña

3. a. lena   b. leña

4. a. suena   b. sueña

5. a. mono   b. moño

C. In Spanish, the letter ch is pronounced like its English equivalent in *church*. Read the following words when you hear the corresponding number, then repeat the correct pronunciation.

1. mucho   4. Chile

2. muchacho   5. mochila

3. Concha   6. hache

D. Dictado. You will hear five sentences. Each will be said twice. Write what you hear.

1. _____

2. _____

3. _____

4. _____

5. _____

MINIDIÁLOGOS Y GRAMÁTICA

32. Talking About the Past (3): Irregular Preterites

A. Minidiálogo: ¿Qué hay en un nombre? You will hear a dialogue followed by a series of statements. Circle **C** if the statement is true or **F** if it is false. If the information is not given, circle **ND** (**no lo dice**).

1. C F ND   Hubo un bautizo en casa de don Pepe ayer.

2. C F ND   Una de las personas que habla no pudo asistir al bautizo.

3. C F ND   A don Pepe no le gusta el nombre de su nieta.

4. C F ND   El nombre de la niña es difícil de pronunciar.

B. Encuesta: Hablando de lo que pasó ayer. You will hear a series of statements about what happened to you yesterday. For each statement, check the appropriate answer. No answers will be given on the tape. The answers you choose should be correct for you!

1. □ Sí   □ No   5. □ Sí   □ No

2. □ Sí   □ No   6. □ Sí   □ No

3. □ Sí   □ No   7. □ Sí   □ No

4. □ Sí   □ No   8. □ Sí   □ No

C. Una fiesta de Nochebuena. Tell what happened at the party, using the written and oral cues.

1. estar en casa de Mario   4. cantar villancicos (*Christmas carols*)

2. tener que limpiar la casa   5. ¡estar estupenda!

3. venir con comida y regalos

D. Descripción: ¿Qué hizo Rodolfo hoy? Tell what Rodolfo did today after you hear the corresponding number for each drawing. Use the verbs and phrases listed. You will hear a possible answer on the tape.

1.    hacer / camas

2.    lavar / ropa

3.    poner / lavaplatos

4.    ir / mercado

5.    traer / comida a casa

E.   Preguntas: ¿Qué hiciste la Navidad pasada? You will hear a series of questions. Each will be said twice. Answer, using the written cues. Use object pronouns when possible.

1.   en casa

2.   sí: venir todos mis tíos y primos

3.   su novia

4.   sí

5.   debajo del árbol

33. Talking About the Past (4): Preterite of Stem-Changing Verbs

A.   Encuesta: Hablando de lo que hicieron ayer. You will hear a series of statements about what people in your class did yesterday. For each statement, check the appropriate answer. No answers will be given on the tape. The answers you choose should be correct for your class!

1. □ Sí   □ No

2. □ Sí   □ No

3. □ Sí   □ No

4. □ Sí   □ No

5. □ Sí   □ No

6. □ Sí   □ No

7. □ Sí   □ No

B.   La fiesta de sorpresa

Paso 1. You will hear a brief paragraph, narrated by Ernesto, about a surprise party. Listen carefully and check the appropriate actions for each person.

PERSONA	VESTIRSE ELEGANTEMENTE	SENTIRSE MAL	DORMIR TODA LA TARDE	PREFERIR QUE-DARSE EN CASA
Julia				
Matilde				
Tomás				
Ernesto (el narrador)				

Paso 2. You will hear a series of statements about the preceding paragraph. Each will be said twice. Circle **C** if the statement is true or **F** if it is false. If the information is not given, circle **ND** (**no lo dice**).

1. C F ND

2. C F ND

3. C F ND

4. C F ND

5. C F ND

Paso 3. Now answer the questions you hear, based on the information from the chart. You will hear each question twice. Check the answers to **Paso 1** in the Appendix before you begin **Paso 3.**

    1. ...   2. ...   3. ...   4. ...

C. La fiesta de despedida de Carmen. You will hear a brief description of a going-away party for Carmen, narrated by Carmen. Then you will hear a series of questions about the party. Answer them, based on the written cues, choosing one verb from each pair.

   1. *decidí / decidió* dejar su puesto

   2. *di / dieron* una fiesta

   3. *empezó / empecé* a llorar

   4. *me reí / se rieron* y *hablé / hablaron* hasta las cinco

   5. *se sintió / me sentí* un poco triste

D. ¿Qué le pasó a Antonio? Tell what happened to Antonio when you hear the corresponding number. First, listen to the beginning of Antonio's story.

   Raquel Morales invitó a Antonio a una fiesta en su casa. Antonio le dijo a la señorita Morales que él iba (*was going*) a traer los refrescos, pero...

   1. no recordar llevar refrescos

   2. perder la dirección de la Srta. Morales

   3. llegar muy tarde a la fiesta

   4. no divertirse

   5. sentirse enfermo después de la fiesta

   6. acostarse muy tarde

   7. dormir mal esa noche

   8. despertarse a las cinco de la mañana

   9. tener que ir al trabajo de todas formas (*anyway*)

34. Expressing Extremes: Superlatives

A. Minidiálogo: Otro aspecto del mundo del trabajo. You will hear a dialogue followed by a series of statements. Circle the number of the statement that best summarizes the dialogue.

   1. The main focus of this conversation is the importance of finding a good job.
   2. The main focus of this conversation is the difficulty of going through an interview.
   3. The main focus of this conversation is someone's dissatisfaction with the job he or she has just left.

B. Encuesta: ¿Está Ud. de acuerdo? You will hear a series of statements. Indicate your opinion by checking the appropriate answer. No answers will be given on the tape. The answers you choose should be correct for you!

1. □ Sí   □ No   □ No tengo opinión.

2. □ Sí   □ No   □ No tengo opinión.

3. □ Sí   □ No   □ No tengo opinión.

4. □ Sí   □ No   □ No tengo opinión.

5. □ Sí   □ No   □ No tengo opinión.

6. □ Sí   □ No   □ No tengo opinión.

7. □ Sí   □ No   □ No tengo opinión.

C. Chismes (*Gossip*) **de la boda de Julia y Patricio.** Your friend's wedding celebration has the best of everything. Answer some questions about it, using the written cues.

> MODELO: (*you hear*) Son elegantes las camisas, ¿verdad? (*you see*) almacén →
> (*you say*) Sí, son las camisas más elegantes del almacén.

1. joyería (*jewelry store*)   4. año

2. fiesta   5. todos los invitados (*guests*)

3. almacén

SITUACIONES

A. In the following conversations you will hear language appropriate for different types of gatherings. Read the conversations silently as you listen.

(*A la llegada*)

> —¡Hola, chicos! ¡Cuánto gusto! Pasen, pasen.
> —¡Hola! Gracias por la invitación, ¿eh?

(*Durante la fiesta*)

> —Otro año… y aquí estamos todos otra vez.
> —Somos más este año, abuela.
> —Eso está bien.

> —Maripepa, te presento a una amiga que está pasando el año en Madrid.
> —Hola. Encantada de estar aquí.
> —¡Qué bien hablas español!

(*A la despedida*)

> —Mañana estamos aquí a las nueve para ayudarte a limpiar la casa.
> —No es necesario. Se lo agredezco, de verdad, pero no…
> —No es molestia.
> —Bueno, si insisten.

B. Now you will hear a series of conversations. Listen carefully and indicate when each conversation might take place: at the beginning of the party, during the party, or at the end of the party.

1. a. a la llegada b. durante la fiesta c. a la despedida

2. a. a la llegada b. durante la fiesta c. a la despedida

3. a. a la llegada b. durante la fiesta c. a la despedida

4. a. a la llegada b. durante la fiesta c. a la despedida

UN POCO DE TODO (PARA ENTREGAR)

A. Un día típico. You will hear a description of a day in Ángela's life, narrated in the past. Then you will hear a series of statements. Circle **C** if the statement is true or **F** if it is false. If the information is not given, circle **ND** (**no lo dice**). First, listen to the statements and try to get an idea of the information for which you need to listen.

1. C F ND Ángela se acostó tarde ayer.

2. C F ND Ángela se levantó a las seis y media.

3. C F ND Ángela se puso furiosa cuando llegó a la oficina.

4. C F ND El jefe le dio mucho trabajo.

5. C F ND Los padres de Ángela viven lejos de ella.

6. C F ND Cuando Ángela se acostó, se durmió inmediatamente.

B. *Listening Passage.* **El carnaval**

Antes de escuchar. You will hear a passage about carnival celebrations. The following words appear in the passage.

pagano	*pagan, not religious*
la Cuaresma	*Lent*
las máscaras	*masks*
los disfraces	*costumes*
caricaturesco	*cartoonish, satirical*
inolvidable	*unforgettable*

Listening Passage. Here is the passage. First, listen to it to get a general idea of the content. Then rewind the tape and listen again for specific information.

Después de escuchar. Indicate the statements that contain information that you *cannot* infer from the listening passage.

1. □ El Carnaval es una tradición exclusivamente europea.

2. □ A pesar de las diferencias, las celebraciones de Carnaval tienen muchas semejanzas (*similarities*).

3. □ El Carnaval celebra la llegada del buen tiempo.

4. □ Los mejores Carnavales se celebran en Europa.

5. □ La gran diferencia entre el Carnaval de Río y los otros Carnavales es que el de Río se celebra en un mes distinto (diferente).

6. ☐ La persona que habla tuvo gran dificultad con el idioma en Río de Janeiro.

7. ☐ La persona que habla quiere ir al Mardi Gras de Nueva Orleáns el próximo año.

Now turn on the tape.

C. ¿Qué hiciste ayer? Using the preterite of the verbs you hear, tell what you did yesterday. Each cue will be said twice. Add any details you need. No answers will be given on the tape. Stop the tape and write the answers.

1. _____

2. _____

3. _____

4. _____

5. _____

6. _____

7. _____

8. _____

D. Y para terminar… Entrevista: Temas varios. You will hear a series of questions. Each will be said twice. Answer, based on your own experience. No answers will be given on the tape. Stop the tape and write the answers.

1. _____

2. _____

3. _____

4. _____

5. _____

6. _____

7. _____

8. _____

CAPÍTULO **11**

VOCABULARIO: PREPARACIÓN

A. Descripción: ¡Qué día más terrible! You will hear a series of sentences. Each will be said twice. Write the letter of each sentence next to the appropriate drawing. First, stop the tape and look at the drawings.

1.

2.

3.

4.

5.

B. Algunas partes del cuerpo. Identify the following body parts when you hear the corresponding number. Begin each sentence with **Es...** or **Son...** , as appropriate.

C. Presiones del trabajo. You have been under a lot of pressure at work and it is affecting your judgment as well as other aspects of your life. Describe what has happened to you, using the oral cues.

MODELO: *(you hear)* no pagar mis cuentas → *(you say)* No pagué mis cuentas.

1. ... 2. ... 3. ... 4. ... 5. ... 6. ...

D. Preguntas personales. You will hear a series of questions about how you do certain things. Answer, using the written cues or your own information. You will hear a possible answer on the tape. First, listen to the cues.

hablar español	hacer cola	salir con mis amigos
jugar al béisbol	escuchar el estéreo	limpiar la estufa
faltar a clase	tocar el piano	

1. ... 2. ... 3. ... 4. ...

LOS HISPANOS HABLAN: RECUERDOS...

In the previous chapter, you heard about Karen's and Xiomara's good memories of their **quinceañeras**. Now you will hear Diana's description of hers. The following words appear in the description.

me salieron mal	*turned out badly for me*
la peluquería	*beauty parlor*
el aguacero	*downpour*
casi se me dañó el peinado	*my hairdo was almost ruined*
no me bajaba	*I couldn't get [it] on*
las mangas	*sleeves*
apretadas	*tight*
se dio cuenta	*he realized*
cambiar pareja	*to change (dance) partners*

Now, stop the tape and check the statements that are true according to the description.

1. □ Cuando Diana salió del salón de belleza, estaba lloviendo.

2. □ Diana tuvo problemas con el vestido.

3. □ Al fotógrafo se le olvidó ponerle película a su cámara.

4. □ Diana llegó temprano a la fiesta.

5. □ Los amigos de Diana bailaron con ella.

6. □ A Diana le gustó mucho su fiesta de quince años.

Now turn on the tape.

PRONUNCIACIÓN Y ORTOGRAFÍA: Y *AND* LL

A. At the beginning of a word or syllable, the Spanish sound [y] is pronounced somewhat like the letter *y* in English *yo-yo* or *papaya*. However, there is no exact English equivalent for this sound. In addition, there are variants of the sound, depending on the country of origin of the speaker.

Listen to these differences:

> el Caribe: Yolanda lleva una blusa amarilla. Yo no.
> España: Yolanda lleva una blusa amarilla. Yo no.
> la Argentina: Yolanda lleva una blusa amarilla. Yo no.

B. Although **y** and **ll** are pronounced exactly the same by most Spanish speakers, in some regions of Spain **ll** is pronounced like the [y] sound in *million*, except that it is one single sound.

Listen to these differences.

> España: Guillermo es de Castilla.
> Sudamérica: Guillermo es de Castilla.

C. Repeat the following words, imitating the speaker.

1. llamo   llueve   yogurt   yate   yanqui   yoga

2. ellas   tortilla   millón   mayo   destruyo   tuyo (*yours*)

D. ¿*Ll* o *l*? You will hear a series of words. Each will be said twice. Circle the letter used to spell each.

1. ll   l   3. ll   l   5. ll   l

2. ll   l   4. ll   l   6. ll   l

E. **Repaso:** *ñ, l, y.* When you hear the corresponding number, read the following sentences. Then listen to the correct pronunciation and say the sentence again.

1. El señor Muñoz es de España y habla español.

2. Yolanda Carrillo es de Castilla.

3. ¿Llueve o no llueve allá en Yucatán?

MINIDIÁLOGOS Y GRAMÁTICA

35. Descriptions and Habitual Actions in the Past: Imperfect of Regular and Irregular Verbs

A. **Minidiálogo: La nostalgia.** You will hear a dialogue followed by a series of statements about the dialogue. Circle **C, F,** or **ND** (**no lo dice**).

1. C F ND   Cuando los hijos eran chiquitos (*small*), había mucho ruido en casa de los abuelos.

2. C F ND   En verano, les gustaba ir a las montañas.

3. C F ND   Armando prefiere los tiempos más tranquilos del presente.

4. C F ND   Durante esta conversación, Armando escuchaba a su esposa con mucha atención.

B. Encuesta: ¿Qué hacías y cómo eras cuando eras joven? You will hear a series of statements about what you used to do or what you were like when you were younger. For each statement, check the appropriate answer. No answers will be given on the tape. The answers you choose should be correct for you!

1. ☐ Sí   ☐ No   4. ☐ Sí   ☐ No   7. ☐ Sí   ☐ No

2. ☐ Sí   ☐ No   5. ☐ Sí   ☐ No   8. ☐ Sí   ☐ No

3. ☐ Sí   ☐ No   6. ☐ Sí   ☐ No   9. ☐ Sí   ☐ No

C. En el aeropuerto: Una despedida

Paso 1. You will hear a description of a farewell between parents and their son, who is leaving home to attend medical school. Listen carefully, and indicate the appropriate actions for each person.

	ESTAR EN EL AEROPUERTO	IR A SAN JOSÉ	ESTAR MUY NERVIOSO/A	ESTAR PREOCUPADO/A	SENTIRSE TRISTE
Gustavo					
la madre de Gustavo					
el padre de Gustavo					

Paso 2. Now you will hear a series of statements about the passage. Each will be said twice. Circle **C** or **F**.

1. C F   2. C F   3. C F   4. C F   5. C F

Paso 3. Now answer the questions you hear, based on the information in your chart. Check the answers for **Paso 1** in the Appendix before you begin **Paso 3**. Each question will be said twice. If you prefer, stop the tape and write the answers.

1. _____

2. _____

3. _____

4. _____

5. _____

D. Describiendo el pasado: En la primaria. Practice telling what you and others used to do in grade school, using the oral and written cues.

1. yo   3. tú   5. nosotros

2. Rodolfo   4. todos   6. Silvia

E. ¿Qué hacían antes? You will hear a series of sentences about present actions. Tell what used to happen, using the written cues.

MODELO: (*you hear*) Ahora enseña química.   (*you see*) matemáticas →
(*you say*) Antes enseñaba matemáticas.

1. California   4. en clase turística

2. muy mal   5. mucho

3. elegantemente

36. Expressing Unplanned or Unexpected Events: Another Use of **se**

A. Encuesta: ¿Cómo eras en la escuela primaria? You will hear a series of questions about what you were like when you were in grade school. For each question, check the appropriate answer. No answers will be given on the tape. The answers you choose should be correct for you!

1. □ Sí   □ No   3. □ Sí   □ No   5. □ Sí   □ No

2. □ Sí   □ No   4. □ Sí   □ No   6. □ Sí   □ No

B. ¡Qué distraído! You will hear a description of Luis, followed by a series of statements about what he forgot to do this morning. Place the number of each statement next to its logical result. First, listen to the results.

a. ___ No va a poder arrancar (*start*) el coche.

b. ___ No va a recibir ningún mensaje (*message*).

c. ___ Es posible que se le queme (*burn down*) el apartamento.

d. ___ Le van a robar la computadora.

e. ___ Lo van a echar (*evict*) de su apartamento.

C. Dictado. You will hear the following sentences. Each will be said twice. Listen carefully and write the missing words.

1. A ellos _____ _____ _____ el número de teléfono de Marta.

2. A Juan _____ _____ _____ las gafas.

3. No quiero que _____ _____ _____ el equipaje en el aeropuerto.

4. A los niños _____ _____ _____ los juguetes.

SITUACIONES

A. Accidentes de la vida diaria. You will hear the following brief dialogues that illustrate how to respond politely in Spanish in different situations. Read the dialogues silently as you listen.

(*En una mesa o dondequiera que sea*)

—¡Oh! Discúlpeme. Permítame que le limpie la camisa.
—No se preocupe. No es nada.
—Lo siento muchísimo.

(*En el autobús o en el metro*)

—Sígueme. Hay un sitio en el fondo.
—¡Hombre! Es imposible llegar allí.
—¿Tú crees? Mira… Con permiso… disculpe, señora, fue sin querer… Con permiso… Perdone…
   Permiso, gracias… ¡Uy! Perdón, lo siento, señora.
—¡Maleducado!

(*Al llegar tarde a una cita*)

—¡Uf! Lo siento. No era mi intención llegar tan tarde. De verdad. Fue culpa del tráfico.
—Anda… No te voy a regañar por diez minutos de retraso. No importa.

(Al olvidar algo)

—Oye, ¿trajiste los apuntes que te pedí?

—¿Los apuntes? ¿Qué apuntes? ¡Ay! Se me olvidó por completo. Lo lamento. Ahora mismo vuelvo a casa para traértelos.

—Bueno, bueno… No es para tanto. Me los traes mañana, ¿eh?

B. Now you will participate in two conversations, partially printed in your manual. Use expressions from the list below. First, listen to the list.

1. ¡Lo siento! Fue sin querer.
2. No se preocupe.
3. Discúlpeme.

1. En la farmacia: Ud. se da con una señora y a ella se le cae el frasco (*jar*) de medicina que llevaba.

SRA.: ¡Ay, no!… ¡el frasco!

UD.: _____ 1

SRA.: ¿Qué voy a hacer? Era una medicina para mi hijito, que está enfermo.

UD.: _____.² Yo le compro otro frasco.

2. En el aeropuerto: Ud. se equivoca y toma el asiento de otra persona. Cuando ésta vuelve, quiere que Ud. le dé su puesto.

SR.: Perdón, pero ése es mi asiento.

UD.: _____.³ Aquí lo tiene.

SR.: Muchas gracias.

UN POCO DE TODO (PARA ENTREGAR)

A. Situaciones delicadas. You will hear four situations. Choose the best response to each.

1. a. ¡Ay, me hice daño en la mano!

   b. ¡Qué mala suerte, Sr. Ramos! ¿Tiene otro vaso?

   c. Lo siento muchísimo, Sr. Ramos. Fue sin querer. ¿Puedo comprarle otro?

2. a. No me importa que no te guste el menú. Vamos a comer aquí.

   b. Lo siento mucho, pero pensé que te gustaría este restaurante. ¿Quieres ir a otro?

   c. Bueno, yo me quedo aquí, pero si tú quieres irte, a mí no me importa.

3. a. Lo siento, viejo, pero no tengo ganas de trabajar más hoy.

   b. Bueno, si Ud. insiste, me quedo a trabajar.

   c. Solamente voy a trabajar tarde si me aumenta el sueldo.

4. a. No se preocupe. Estoy bien.

   b. Mire, señor, si sus niños no dejan de (*don't stop*) hacer tanto ruido, voy a llamar a la policía.

   c. Por favor, señor, dígales a sus niños que no hagan tanto ruido… ¡Tengo un dolor de cabeza tremendo!

B. *Listening Passage:* **Primeras impresiones**

Antes de escuchar. You will hear a passage in which a person who is now living in this country tells about her first impressions of people in the United States. The following words and phrases appear in the passage.

las amistades	los amigos
aumentó	*increased*
judío	*Jewish*
para que yo pudiera	*so that I could*
maravilloso	*marvelous, wonderful*
para que yo tuviera	*so that I would have*
los Reyes Magos de Oriente	*Three Wise Men* (*Magi*)
echo de menos	*I miss*
el pueblo	*people*

Listening Passage. Here is the passage. First, listen to it to get a general idea of the content. Then rewind the tape and listen again for specific information.

Después de escuchar. Circle the best answer to each of the following questions. **¡OJO!** There may be more than one answer for some items.

1. Es probable que la persona que habla sea de…

   a. España   b. los Estados Unidos   c. Latinoamérica   d. No lo dice.

2. Al principio (*beginning*), esta persona pensaba que los estadounidenses eran…

   a. abiertos   b. corteses   c. fríos   d. relajados

3. La amiga que invitó a esta persona a su casa era…

   a. protestante   b. judía   c. ateísta   d. católica

4. Antes de visitar a la familia de Abi, la narradora…

   a.   no conocía Nueva York

   b.   compró regalos

   c.   pasaba la Navidad con su familia

   d.   no sabía mucho de las tradiciones judías

5. La familia de Abi no entendía…

   a.   español

   b.   la tradición de Navidad

   c.   por qué se dan regalos el seis de enero

   d.   por qué la narradora no tenía muchos amigos

6. Ahora, la estudiante hispana piensa que…

   a.   los estadounidenses son gente fría

   b.   los estadounidenses no se besan lo suficiente

   c.   los estadounidenses no saben nada de las tradiciones hispanas

   d.   los estadounidenses demuestran el cariño de una manera distinta a la de los hispanos

Now turn on the tape.

C. Entrevista: Temas varios. You will hear a series of questions. Each will be said twice. Answer, based on your own experience. Stop the tape and write the answers.

1. _____
2. _____
3. _____
4. _____
5. _____
6. *Se me...* _____

D. Y para terminar... Una canción. The following song is popular among Spanish university students.

Pim-pi-ri-rim-pim-pím

A mí me gusta el pim-pi-ri-rim-pim-pím
Con la botella empiná-pa-ra-ra-pa-pá.°   *tilted, raised*
Con el pim-pi-ri-rim-pim-pím,
Con el pa-pa-ra-ra-pa-pá.
Al que no le gusta el vino es un animal,
Es un animal...
...O no tiene un real.°   *coin (money)*

CAPÍTULO 12

VOCABULARIO: PREPARACIÓN

A. Encuesta: Hablando de la salud. You will hear a series of statements about your health habits. For each statement, check the appropriate answer. No answers will be given on the tape. The answers you choose should be correct for you!

1. ☐ Sí ☐ No   4. ☐ Sí ☐ No   7. ☐ Sí ☐ No

2. ☐ Sí ☐ No   5. ☐ Sí ☐ No   8. ☐ Sí ☐ No

3. ☐ Sí ☐ No   6. ☐ Sí ☐ No

B. Encuesta: Opiniones. You will hear a series of statements about health habits. Indicate your opinion by checking the appropriate answers. No answers will be given on the tape. The answers you choose should be correct for you!

	ESTOY DE ACUERDO	NO ESTOY DE ACUERDO	NO TENGO OPINIÓN
1.	☐	☐	☐
2.	☐	☐	☐
3.	☐	☐	☐
4.	☐	☐	☐
5.	☐	☐	☐
6.	☐	☐	☐
7.	☐	☐	☐
8.	☐	☐	☐

C. Asociaciones. You will hear a series of activities. Each will be said twice. Circle the body part that you associate with each. ¡OJO! There may be more than one answer for each activity.

1.	los pies	las piernas	los dientes	la garganta
2.	los pulmones	las manos	la nariz	los ojos
3.	los pulmones	la boca	las manos	las piernas
4.	los dientes	la garganta	el corazón	la boca
5.	los ojos	los pulmones	las piernas	el estómago

D. Algunas partes del cuerpo. Identify the following body parts when you hear the corresponding number. Use **Es...** or **Son...** and the appropriate definite article.

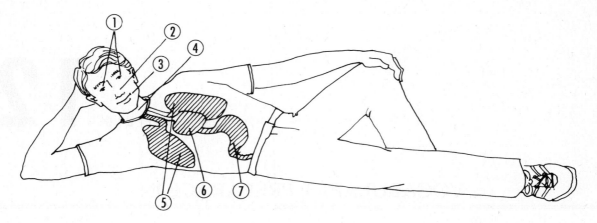

1. ...   2. ...   3. ...   4. ...   5. ...   6. ...   7. ...

E. Para completar. You will hear a series of incomplete statements. Each will be said twice. Circle the letter of the word or phrase that best completes each statement.

1. a. ponerle una inyección   b. respirar bien

2. a. los ojos   b. el corazón

3. a. una tos   b. un jarabe

4. a. las pastillas verdes   b. esta receta para el antibiótico

5. a. frío   b. un resfriado

F. En el consultorio de la doctora Vásquez: ¿Qué debo hacer para tener buena salud? You are a doctor whose patient wants to know what he should do to be in good health. Tell him what to do or what *not* to do, using the oral cues. Use formal commands, as in the model.

MODELO: (*you hear*) hacer ejercicio → (*you say*) Haga ejercicio.

1. ...   2. ...   3. ...   4. ...   5. ...   6. ...

LOS HISPANOS HABLAN:
¿PRACTICAS UN DEPORTE? ¿POR QUÉ?

Paso 1. You will hear several Hispanic students tell about the sports they play and why. The first time you listen, write the name of the sport or sports played by each student. Then, listen again and jot down each person's reasons for choosing the sport. The following words appear in the passages.

emocionante	*exciting*
entretenido	*entertaining, fun*
que uno se engorde	*that one get fat*
habilidad y destreza	*ability and skill*

	DEPORTE(S)	RAZÓN POR LA CUAL SE PRACTICA
Clara		
Antonio		
Gabriela		
Patricia		
Teresa		
José		
Xiomara		
Erick		

Paso 2. Now stop the tape and answer these questions, based on the chart. Check your answers to **Paso 1** in the Appendix before you begin **Paso 2.**

1. ¿Qué deporte es más popular entre los estudiantes que contestaron las preguntas?

   _____

2. ¿Cuántas personas mencionaron entre sus razones la salud o los beneficios para el cuerpo?

   _____

Now turn on the tape.

PRONUNCIACIÓN Y ORTOGRAFÍA: X, N

A. The letter **x** is usually pronounced [ks], as in English. Before a consonant, however, it is often pronounced [s]. Repeat the following words, imitating the speaker.

1. [ks]   léxico   sexo   axial   existen   examen
2. [s]   explican   extraordinario   extremo   sexto   extraterrestre
3. ¿Piensas que existen los extraterrestres?

   ¡Nos explican que es algo extraordinario!

   No me gustan las temperaturas extremas.

   La medicina no es una ciencia exacta.

B. Before **p, b, v,** and **m,** the letter **n** is pronounced [m]. Before [k], [g], and [x], **n** is pronounced like the [ng] sound in the English word *sing*. In all other positions, **n** is pronounced as it is in English.

Repeat the following words and phrases, imitating the speaker.

1. [m]   convence   un beso   un peso   con Manuel   con Pablo

         en Perú   en Venezuela   en México   son buenos

2. [ng] en casa   en Castilla   un general   son generosos

         son jóvenes   en Quito   en Granada   con Juan

37. Narrating in the Past: Using the Preterite and Imperfect

A. Dictado: Minidiálogo: Un resfriado muy grave. You will hear a dialogue between a nurse and a patient. Listen carefully and write the missing words. Then you will hear a series of statements. Circle the letter of the person who might have made each statement.

ENFERMERA: ¿Cuándo _____¹ a sentirse mal?

RODRIGO: Ayer por la noche _____² un poco congestionado. _____³ mucho y me _____⁴ todo el cuerpo. Hoy, cuando me _____,⁵ me _____⁶ peor todavía. Por eso _____⁷ para hacer una cita.

ENFERMERA: ¿Tiene otros síntomas?

RODRIGO: Creo que anoche _____⁸ un poco de fiebre, pero no estoy seguro. No me _____⁹ la temperatura. No _____¹⁰ termómetro.

ENFERMERA: Pues... ¡Nosotros sí tenemos! Abra la boca, por favor.

1. a. el paciente   b. la enfermera
2. a. el paciente   b. la enfermera
3. a. el paciente   b. la enfermera
4. a. el paciente   b. la enfermera
5. a. el paciente   b. la enfermera

B. Condiciones y acciones: De viaje. You will hear a series of situations. Each will be said twice. Write the number of each situation next to the logical action. First, listen to the list of actions.

a. ___ Por eso llegué tarde al aeropuerto.

b. ___ Por eso pedí asiento en la sección de no fumar.

c. ___ Por eso lo facturé.

d. ___ Por eso pedí un vuelo directo.

e. ___ Por eso compré un boleto de ida y vuelta.

C. ¿Un sábado típico? You will hear a series of sentences that describe a series of events. Form new sentences, using the written cues. Begin each sentence with **El sábado pasado...**

MODELO: (*you hear*) Todos los sábados, Carlos se despertaba a las siete. (*you see*) ocho →
(*you say*) El sábado pasado, se despertó a las ocho.

1. mercado   2. café   3. hermana   4. después de la cena   5. tarde

D. Una decisión difícil

Paso 1. You will hear the following sentences about Laura's decision to leave her hometown. Then, when you hear the cue in parentheses, restate the sentences, changing the italicized verbs to the preterite or imperfect, as appropriate. In each case, you will insert the cue at the beginning of the sentence. In this exercise, you will practice narrating in the past.

> MODELO: (*you see and hear*) *Vivimos* en un pequeño pueblo en las montañas. (de niños) →
> (*you say*) De niños, vivíamos en un pequeño pueblo en las montañas.

1. Mi madre *trabaja* en una panadería (*bakery*). (los martes y los jueves)

2. Mi padre *trabaja* en una tienda de comestibles (*food store*). (todos los días)

3. *Vamos* a la ciudad y *compramos* cosas que no *podemos* encontrar en nuestro pueblo.

   (frecuentemente)

4. *Consigo* trabajo permanente en la ciudad y *decido* dejar mi pueblo para siempre. (un verano)

5. *Empiezo* a tomar clases de noche en la universidad y *dejo* mi puesto permanente por uno de

   tiempo parcial. (al año siguiente)

6. Mis padres *están* tristes porque yo no *vivo* con ellos, pero ahora están contentos con mi decisión.

   (antes)

Paso 2. Answer the questions you hear, based on the preceding story. Each question will be said twice.

   1. ... 2. ... 3. ... 4. ... 5. ... 6. ...

E. Preguntas. Practice telling how you felt today by answering a series of questions. Each will be said twice. Answer in the affirmative or negative, as indicated by the written cues.

   1. sí 2. no 3. sí 4. sí 5. sí

F. Descripción. Tell what the following people are doing when you hear the corresponding number. Follow the model. You will hear a possible answer on the tape.

> MODELO: (*you see*) cocinar / mientras / poner la mesa →
> (*you say*) Luis cocinaba mientras Paula ponía la mesa.

1. leer / cuando / entrar

2. cantar / mientras / tocar el piano

3. llorar / mientras / ponerle una inyección

4. jugar / cuando / pegarle

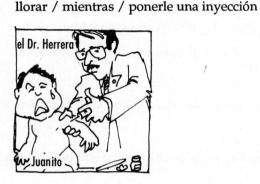

38. Recognizing **que, quien(es), lo que:** Relative Pronouns

A. Minidiálogo: Lo que dijo el Dr. Matamoros. You will hear a dialogue followed by a series of statements. Write the letter of the person who might have made each statement next to the statement. *Note:* **cobrar** = *to charge for a service.*

a = Beatriz   b = su amiga Isabel   c = el Dr. Matamoros

1. ___ Te digo lo mismo que el médico y no te cobro nada.

2. ___ Tuve que ir al médico porque no me sentía bien.

3. ___ La examiné y le dije que tenía que guardar cama.

4. ___ Le cobré sesenta dólares por la visita.

B. Por teléfono. Tell the receptionist at the hospital with whom you wish to speak, following the model. Use the phrase **con quien** in each sentence.

MODELO: (*you hear*) el señor Rubio →
(*you say*) El señor Rubio es la persona con quien quiero hablar.

1. ... 2. ... 3. ... 4. ...

C. En el consultorio. Imagine that you are Dr. Sotelo. Explain to a nurse what you need and where it is located, following the model.

> MODELO: (*you hear*) termómetro (*you see*) armario →
> (*you say*) Necesito el termómetro que está en mi armario.

1. mi bolsa 2. mi consultorio 3. mi escritorio 4. ese pueblo

SITUACIONES

A. Hablando con la doctora. You will hear a conversation between a patient and a doctor. Read it silently as you listen.

ENFERMERA: ¿David Gonzáles? Pase Ud. al consultorio de la doctora, por favor, y siéntese. La doctora lo verá pronto.

DAVID: Gracias.

DOCTORA: Buenos días, David. ¿Cómo está? ¿Qué tiene hoy?

DAVID: Tengo un resfriado fatal. Toso tanto por la noche que no puedo dormir bien.

DOCTORA: Parece que todos están resfriados esta semana. Vamos a ver. Saque la lengua. Abra bien la boca y diga: «Aaaaa… ».

DAVID: Aaaaaa.

DOCTORA: La garganta está un poco inflamada. Ahora respire profundamente. Diga: «Treinta y tres».

DAVID: Treinta y tres.

DOCTORA: Bien. Ud. no tiene nada serio en los pulmones.

DAVID: Pero toso mucho, doctora. Ya tosía antes de resfriarme.

DOCTORA: Lo que pasa es que fuma demasiado. Ahora calle mientras le ausculto el corazón. Hmm… ¿Hace Ud. mucho ejercicio físico?

DAVID: Fui campeón de natación en el colegio.

DOCTORA: Bueno, en general, Ud. está en muy buen estado físico.

DAVID: ¿Y para este resfriado?

DOCTORA: Pues, unas aspirinas y… paciencia. Y deje de fumar, ¿eh?

B. Now you will participate in a conversation, partially printed in your manual, about another illness. You will take the role of the patient. Complete it with the following cues. If you prefer, stop the tape and write the answers. Here are the cues for your conversation:

1. tener dolor de cabeza
2. estar muy cansado/a
3. tres días
4. no tener fiebre

DOCTORA: Siéntese, por favor. ¿Qué le ocurre?

UD.: Bueno, _____ [1] y

_____.[2]

DOCTORA: ¿Cuánto tiempo hace que tiene estos síntomas?

UD.: Hace _____.[3]

DOCTORA: Bueno, le voy a tomar la temperatura. Si tiene fiebre, le voy a recomendar que guarde cama por uno o dos días y que tome un antibiótico.

UD.: Y, ¿si _____ [4]?

DOCTORA: Entonces le voy a recomendar que tenga paciencia. Es posible que sólo sea un resfriado.

A. En el periódico: La salud. You will hear the following ads from Hispanic newspapers. Listen to them and circle the Spanish words or phrases that express the following. First, stop the tape and scan the list of English words.

Deje de fumar

1. killers

2. medical treatment

3. a drug

Lentes de contacto

4. a replacement pair   5. immediate replacement   6. soft or flexible

B. *Listening Passage:* **El sistema médico en los países hispanos**

Antes de escuchar. Stop the tape and do the following prelistening exercise. Read the following statements about medical systems. Check those that you think apply only to the United States.

1. ☐ El sistema médico está controlado por el gobierno.

2. ☐ Hay una gran cantidad de compañías de seguro (*insurance companies*).

3. ☐ Hay menos compañías de seguro.

4. ☐ Cada persona paga los gastos médicos de acuerdo con (*according to*) su salario y no de acuerdo con el tipo de seguro que tiene.

4. ☐ Cualquier (*Any*) persona tiene derecho (*right*) al mejor tratamiento médico posible.

6. ☐ Hay muchas personas que no tienen acceso al tratamiento médico, ya sea (*be it*) por falta de dinero o porque no tienen seguro.

7. ☐ A veces, es necesario esperar mucho tiempo para ver al médico.

8. ☐ A veces hay mucha demanda, pero hay pocos servicios y personal disponibles (*available*).

Now turn on the tape.

Listening Passage. Now you will hear a passage about the medical systems in most of the Hispanic world. The following words and phrases appear in the passage.

el gobierno	*government*
las compañías de seguro	*insurance companies*
proveen	*they provide*
la cobertura	*coverage*
innegable	*undeniable*
la capacidad económica	*economic ability to pay*
el impuesto	*tax*
imprescindible	*indispensable*
tiende a disminuir	*tends to diminish or reduce*
el quebradero de cabeza	*problem, something that requires great thought*

Después de escuchar. You will hear a series of statements. Each will be said twice. Circle **C** or **F**.

1. C F   2. C F   3. C F   4. C F   5. C F

C. Descripción. The captions for the following cartoon will be read on the tape. Listen carefully, then answer the questions about the cartoon. Stop the tape and write the answers. First, listen to the following expressions that appear in the cartoon.

levantado	*up, out of bed*
me he sacado de encima	*I got rid of*
la gripe	*flu*

1. _____

2. _____

3. _____

4. _____

5. _____

6. _____

D. Entrevista: Preguntas personales. You will hear a series of questions. Each will be said twice. Answer, based on your own experience. No answers will be given on the tape. Stop the tape and write the answers.

Hablando de la niñez (*childhood*)

1. _____

2. _____

3. _____

Hablando de la salud

4. _____

5. _____

6. _____

E. Y para terminar... Una canción. «**Triste estaba el Rey David**» is a 15th-century Spanish song written by Alonso de Mudarra.

Triste estaba el Rey David

Triste estaba el Rey David,
Triste y con gran pasión,
Cuando le vinieron nuevas°   *news*
De la muerte° de Absalón.°   *death / son of David*

Cuando le vinieron nuevas
De la muerte de Absalón,
Palabras triste decía,
Salidas del corazón.°   Salidas... Que venían del corazón

REPASO **4**

A. *Listening Passage:* **Un accidente (Para entregar).** You will hear a conversation between a person who has just had an accident and a person who was on the scene. First, listen to get a general idea of the content. Then rewind the tape and listen again for specific information.

Después de escuchar. You will hear a series of questions. Each will be said twice. Not all the questions are based on details of the conversation. Some will ask for your opinion. Stop the tape and write the answers. The following words and expressions appear in the questions.

perdió el conocimiento	*became unconscious*
el accidentado	la víctima del accidente

1. _____

2. _____

3. _____

4. _____

5. _____

B. En la fiesta del Año Nuevo. When you hear the corresponding number, describe what happened at your friend Mateo's New Year's Eve party. Use the following groups of words in the order given, and add any necessary words. ¡OJO! You will be using preterite and imperfect verb forms.

1. todos / llegar / nueve

2. Lisbet / traer / entremeses / vino

3. Rafael y yo / venir tarde / porque / perder / dirección / Mateo

4. Mateo / estar / contentísimo / porque / venir / su novia

5. todos / bailar / mientras / Tito / poner / discos

6. ser / tres / cuando / por fin / terminar / fiesta

C. Situaciones y reacciones. You will hear a series of situations. Each will be said twice. Using the written cues, tell how you would react to each. **¡OJO!** In some cases you will need to supply an appropriate emotion.

> MODELO: (*you hear*) Su compañero de cuarto hizo mucho ruido anoche. ¿Cómo reaccionó Ud.?
> (*you see*) enojarse… porque yo / querer dormir → (*you say*) Me enojé porque yo quería dormir.

1. ponerse… porque yo / necesitar un coche

2. quedarse en casa… porque (yo) / ya no tener ganas de ir a la playa

3. ponerse… porque yo / tener que leer una novela para una clase

4. ponerse… porque lo que yo decía de ella / no ser bueno

D. Descripción: Escenas de la vida diaria. When you hear the corresponding number, tell what the following people were doing when something else happened. Base your answer on the written cues. You will hear a possible answer on the tape.

> MODELO: (*you see*) preparar / entrar →
> (*you say*) Rita estaba preparando la comida cuando entró Nuria.

1. limpiar / llegar

2. tomar / entrar

3.   leer / entrar

4.   bañarse / sonar

E.   Conversación: En el consultorio de la doctora Rubio (Para entregar). You have been feeling ill for three days. You have a fever, a cough, and you feel nauseous. Using these symptoms and any other logical ones, complete the following conversation with Dr. Rubio. First, listen to the conversation.

DRA. RUBIO: Buenas tardes. Pase Ud.

UD.:   _____

DRA. RUBIO: Dígame lo que le ocurre, por favor.

UD.:   _____

DRA. RUBIO: ¿Y cuánto tiempo hace que se siente así?

UD.:   _____

DRA. RUBIO: Bueno, parece que también tiene dificultad en respirar… ¿Le duelen los pulmones cuando respira?

UD.:   _____

DRA. RUBIO: Le voy a dar una receta para un antibiótico y para un jarabe para la tos. Quiero que tome muchos líquidos: agua, té, jugos de fruta… y que descanse. Guarde cama el resto de la semana. Si no está mejor en siete días, llámeme. Hasta luego, y ¡que se mejore pronto!

UD.:   _____

Now turn on the tape.

F.   Descripción: Una fiesta desastrosa (Para entregar). You will hear a series of statements about the following drawing. Each will be said twice. Circle **C** or **F.**

1. C F   2. C F   3. C F   4. C F   5. C F

G. Entrevista (Para entregar). You will hear a series of questions. Each will be said twice. Answer, based on your own experience. Stop the tape and write the answers.

Hablando de la niñez

1. _____

2. _____

3. _____

Hablando de días festivos

4. _____

5. _____

6. _____

Hablando de la salud

7. _____

8. _____

9. _____

CAPÍTULO 13

VOCABULARIO: PREPARACIÓN

A. Encuesta: ¿Cómo manejas? You will hear a series of questions about your driving habits. For each question, check the appropriate answer. No answers will be given on the tape. The answers you choose should be correct for you!

	SIEMPRE	A VECES	¡NUNCA!
1.	☐	☐	☐
2.	☐	☐	☐
3.	☐	☐	☐
4.	☐	☐	☐
5.	☐	☐	☐
6.	☐	☐	☐
7.	☐	☐	☐
8.	☐	☐	☐
9.	☐	☐	☐

B. Definiciones: Hablando de coches. You will hear a series of statements. Each will be said twice. Circle the letter of the word that is best defined by each.

1. a. la batería   b. la gasolina   c. la licencia
2. a. la licencia   b. el camino   c. el taller
3. a. el parabrisas   b. los frenos   c. el semáforo
4. a. la esquina   b. la carretera   c. la llanta
5. a. el accidente   b. el aceite   c. el taller

C. Identifcaciones. Identify the following items when you hear the corresponding number. Begin each sentence with **Es un...**, **Es una...**, or **Son...**

D. Descripción. You will hear a series of statements about the preceding drawing. Circle **C** or **F**.

1. C F   2. C F   3. C F   4. C F   5. C F   6. C F

E. ¿Qué hizo el mecánico? You will hear a series of car problems. Each will be said twice. Using the expressions from the following list, tell what the mechanic did to fix them. First, listen to the list.

arreglar los frenos   revisar la batería
llenar el tanque   cambiar las llantas

1. ...   2. ...   3. ...   4. ...

F. Poniendo las cosas en orden

Paso 1. You will hear a series of questions. Each will be said twice. Circle the correct answer.

1. febrero	enero	junio	abril
2. julio	agosto	octubre	diciembre
3. lunes	jueves	sábado	martes
4. Michael Jordan	Sinead O'Connor	Neil Armstrong	Raúl Julia

Paso 2. Now stop the tape and write a sentence, using ordinal numbers, about each of the answers you circled. Number four is done for you.

1. _____

2. _____

3. _____

4. *La primera persona que caminó en la luna fue Neil Armstrong.*
_____

Now turn on the tape.

G. Descripción: ¿En qué piso… ? You will be asked to tell on what floor a number of families live or on which floor businesses are located. Each question will be said twice. Answer, based on the following drawing. First, stop the tape and look at the drawing.

1. …
2. …
3. …
4. …
5. …
6. …
7. …

= 6

= 5

= 4

= 3

= 2

= 1

= la planta baja

LOS HISPANOS HABLAN: ¿HAY ALGÚN OBJETO QUE TENGA MUCHA IMPORTANCIA EN LA VIDA DIARIA DE TU FAMILIA?

Listen to the answers several students gave to this question. Take notes, if you wish, as you listen. Then check the statements that are true, based on what you heard. The following words appear in the students' answers.

desplazarse	*ir*
la pérdida	*loss*
cualquier inconveniente	*any inconvenience (small problem)*

Apuntes (*Notes*):

_____

_____

(Continúa.)

_____

_____

_____

Now stop the tape and indicate the statements that are true.

1. □ De los estudiantes que respondieron a la pregunta, la mayoría dijo que el auto es el objeto más importante.

2. □ Para una de las personas, los libros eran muy importantes.

3. □ Según los estudiantes, la función del auto era principalmente para ir de paseo y para divertirse.

4. □ Muchos mencionaron que el teléfono también era importante.

Now turn on the tape.

PRONUNCIACIÓN Y ORTOGRAFÍA: *REVIEW OF LINKING*

A. Repeat the following phrases and sentences, pronouncing them as if they were one word.

1. el‿abuelo el‿hijo el‿elefante el‿otoño

2. los‿errores los‿hoteles las‿asistentes las‿ideas

3. con‿Eduardo son‿interesantes en‿Alemania

4. de‿usted para‿ella la‿invitación mi‿abuelo

5. mi‿hijo me‿escuchan la‿arregló lo‿oyó entre‿ellos

6. ¿Qué‿es‿esto?

Tienen‿un‿hijo‿y‿una‿hija.

Aquí‿hay‿ocho‿estudiantes.

Viven‿así‿en‿el‿Ecuador.

B. Dictado. You will hear four sentences. Each will be said twice. Listen carefully and write what you hear.

1. _____

2. _____

3. _____

4. _____

MINIDIÁLOGOS Y GRAMÁTICA

39. Expressing Uncertainty: Use of the Subjunctive: Doubt and Denial

A. Comentarios sobre un coche. You will hear a series of statements about the drawing. Each will be said twice. Circle **C** or **F**.

1. C F
2. C F
3. C F

B. ¿Indicativo o subjuntivo? You will hear a series of sentences. Each will be said twice. Tell whether the sentence expresses certainty (indicative) or doubt (subjunctive).

1. a. certainty   b. doubt   3. a. certainty   b. doubt

2. a. certainty   b. doubt   4. a. certainty   b. doubt

C. ¡Mi coche no funciona! Practice telling what you should do when your car doesn't work well, using the oral and written cues.

> MODELO: (*you see*) Llevo el auto al taller.   (*you hear*) es posible →
> (*you say*) Es posible que lleve el auto al taller.

1. Es un auto viejo, pero…

2. El mecánico lo puede arreglar.

3. Sí, pero te cobran (*they'll charge*) mucho.

4. Bueno, puedo manejarlo así, en estas condiciones.

5. Los frenos funcionan perfectamente.

6. No debes manejarlo así. Tienes razón.

D. ¿Qué piensa Ud.? Your friend Josefina has made a series of statements. You will hear each one twice. Respond to each, using the written cues.

> MODELO: (*you hear*) Juan trae los contratos.   (*you see*) No creo… →
> (*you say*) No creo que Juan traiga los contratos.

1. No creo…   3. Dudo…   5. ¡Qué lástima… !

2. Es verdad…   4. Es increíble… 6. No dudo…

E. Observaciones. You will hear a series of statements about the following drawings. Each will be said twice. React to each statement, according to the model. Begin each answer with **Es verdad que...** or **No es verdad que...**

MODELO: (*you hear*) Amalia tiene un auto nuevo. →
(*you say*) No es verdad que Amalia tenga un auto nuevo.

Amalia

1.

2.

3.

4.

5.

40. Expressing Influence, Emotion, Doubt, and Denial: Uses of the Subjunctive: A Summary

A. Minidiálogo: En el taller. You will hear a dialogue followed by a series of statements. Write the letter of the person who might have made each statement next to the appropriate statement.

a = cliente   b = empleado

1. ___ Acabo de ponerle una batería nueva.

2. ___ Va a ser necesario que Ud. deje su carro aquí.

3. ___ Le voy a revisar las llantas y las bujías (*spark plugs*).

4. ___ Regreso en dos horas para recoger el carro.

B. Comprando un coche. Form new sentences, using the oral cues.

1. (*you see and hear*) ¿Qué quiere Ud. que haga el vendedor?
    (*you hear*) enseñarme los útlimos modelos →
    (*you say*) Quiero que me enseñe los últimos modelos.

    a. ...   b. ...   c. ...

2. (*you see and hear*) ¿Qué es lo que le sorprende?   (*you hear*) (costar tanto los coches) →
    (*you say*) Me sorprende que cuesten tanto los coches.

    a. ...   b. ...   c. ...

41. El infinitivo: Verb + Infinitive; Verb + Preposition + Infinitive: A Summary

A. Ventajas y desventajas de la era de la tecnología. You will hear the following cartoon caption. Then you will hear a series of statements. Circle **C** or **F**.

1. C   F   2. C   F   3. C   F

—Yo quería ir a su oficina a pagar la tasa de estacionamiento,[a] pero no pude hacerlo porque no encontré sitio para estacionar.

[a]tasa... *parking fee*

B. ¿Qué hacen sus amigos? Answer the question by completing the following sentences, according to the oral cues. **¡OJO!** You will need to add words, as in the model.

> MODELO: (*you see*) Me invitan...   (*you hear*) salir con ellos →
> (*you say*) Me invitan a salir con ellos.

1. Me ayudan...   2. Me invitan...   3. Insisten...   4. Tratan...

C. Situaciones. You will hear a series of situations. Answer, using phrases from the list. **¡OJO!** Not all phrases will be used. First, listen to the list.

explicarle lo que pasó
limpiar el parabrisas
ponerles cadenas (*chains*) a las llantas

llevarlo al taller
llamar al médico

1. ...   2. ...   3. ...   4. ...

SITUACIONES

A. Hablando de coches. You will hear three dialogues about getting service at a gas station. Read the dialogues silently as you listen.

(*Un servicio extraordinario*)

E: Buenas. ¿Qué desea?
C: Necesito que me arreglen la llanta de repuesto.
E: Puede dejarla y pasar mañana a recogerla.
C: Pero… salgo de viaje ahora mismo… y quisiera tenerla en seguida.
E: De acuerdo. Se lo hacemos en diez minutos.

(*El servicio normal*)

C: Buenos días.
E: Buenos días. ¿Le lleno el tanque?
C: Sí, primero haga eso, pero después necesito que revise el agua del radiador y el aceite, por favor.
E: Sí, cómo no.

E: ¿En qué puedo servirle?
C: Lléneme el tanque, por favor.
E: ¿Quiere que le revise el aceite?
C: Sí, por favor, y el agua de la batería y del radiador. Y otra cosa, ¿podría mirarme la presión de las ruedas?
E: De acuerdo. Lleve el coche allí delante. Voy en seguida.

B. Now you will participate in a similar conversation, partially printed in your manual, about asking for service at a gas station. Complete it, using the cues in the order given. (If you wish, stop the tape and write the answers.)

Here are the cues for your conversation.

1. revisarme el aceite   2. llenarme el tanque   3. arreglarme la llanta de repuesto

—¿En qué puedo servirle?

—Necesito que Ud. _____ 1

—¿Quiere que le mire la presión de las llantas?

—Sí, por favor, y también quiero que _____ 2

  y que _____ 3

—Sí, cómo no.

UN POCO DE TODO (PARA ENTREGAR)

A. Se venden coches nuevos y usados. You will hear three ads for automobiles. Listen and complete the following sentences by writing the number of the ad in the appropriate space. First, stop the tape and read the incomplete statements.

Dudo que el coche del anuncio número ___ sea una ganga.

El auto del anuncio número ___ es un auto pequeño y económico.

Es probable que el coche del anuncio número ___ gaste mucha gasolina.

Now turn on the tape.

B. *Listening Passage:* **Los coches**

Antes de escuchar. You will hear a passage about the types of cars driven in the Hispanic world. The following words appear in the passage.

la molestia	*bother*
la ayuda	*something helpful*
la clase media-baja	*lower middle class*

Listening Passage. Here is the passage. First, listen to it to get a general idea of the content. Then rewind the tape and listen again for specific information.

Después de escuchar. You will hear a series of statements. Each will be said twice. Circle **C** or **F**. Then stop the tape and correct the statements that are false, according to the passage.

1. C F _____

2. C F _____

3. C F _____

4. C F _____

5. C F _____

Now turn on the tape.

C. En el extranjero: Se venden y se alquilan coches. You will hear the following ad. Then you will hear a series of statements about the ad. Circle **C** or **F**. The following words appear in the ad.

cualquier	*any other*
la fábrica	*factory*
la aduana	*customs duty, fee*
S.A. (Sociedad Anónima)	*Incorporated (Inc.)*

¿VIAJA USTED A ESPAÑA?

COMPRE SU BMW, MERCEDES, VOLVO, VOLKSWAGEN

O cualquier otra marca europea a estricto precio de fábrica.
¡Sin impuestos! ¡Sin aduana! ¡Alquilamos para períodos cortos,
coches nuevos, y tarifas especialísimas!

¡HAGA SU RESERVA YA! ESCRÍBANOS A

REPINTER, S.A.
Capitán Haya, 35. 28020 MADRID. Teléfonos 456 48 08-48 12-48 16

---

1. C F   2. C F   3. C F   4. C F

D. En el periódico: Venta de autos. The following ads appeared in an Argentinian newspaper. Stop the tape, read them, and decide which car you want to buy. Then you will hear a series of questions. Each will be said twice. Answer them, according to the ad you chose. If the information requested in the question is not in the ad, answer with **No lo dice.**

1. _____
2. _____
3. _____
4. _____

E. Entrevista. You will hear a series of questions. Each will be said twice. Answer, based on your own experience. No answers will be given on the tape. Stop the tape and write the answers.

1. _____
2. _____
3. _____
4. _____
5. _____
6. _____
7. _____

F. Y para terminar… Una canción. "Cu cu ru cu cu" is a traditional Mexican folk song.

Cu cu ru cu cu

Dicen que por las noches no más se le iba° en puro llorar.
Dicen que no comía, no más se le iba en puro tomar.
Juran que el mismo cielo se estremecía al oír su llanto.°
Cómo sufría por ella, que hasta en su muerte la fue llamando:
Ay, ay, ay, ay, ay, cantaba.
Ay, ay, ay, ay, ay, gemía.°
Ay, ay, ay, ay, ay, cantaba.
De pasión mortal moría.
Cu cu ru cu cu,
cu cu ru cu cu,
cu cu ru cu cu.
Paloma,° ya no le llores.

no… pasaba su tiempo

Juran… *They swear that even the heavens were touched by his grief.*
he moaned

Dove

CAPÍTULO **14**

VOCABULARIO: PREPARACIÓN

A. Encuestas

Paso 1. Hablando de nuestro ambiente. You will hear a series of statements. For each statement, check the appropriate answer. No answers will be given on the tape. The answers you choose should be correct for you!

1. □ Sí   □ No   5. □ Sí   □ No

2. □ Sí   □ No   6. □ Sí   □ No

3. □ Sí   □ No   7. □ Sí   □ No

4. □ Sí   □ No   8. □ Sí   □ No

Paso 2. Hablando de nuestra ciudad. You will hear a series of statements about the city in which you live. For each statement, check the appropriate answer. No answers will be given on the tape. The answers you choose should be correct for you!

1. □ Sí   □ No   5. □ Sí   □ No

2. □ Sí   □ No   6. □ Sí   □ No

3. □ Sí   □ No   7. □ Sí   □ No

4. □ Sí   □ No   8. □ Sí   □ No

Paso 3. ¿Qué opina sobre el medio ambiente? You will hear a series of statements about environmental concerns. Express your opinion about the issues by checking the appropriate boxes. No answers will be given on the tape. The answers you choose should be correct for you!

	SÍ ENFÁTICO	SÍ	NO TENGO OPINIÓN	NO	NO ENFÁTICO
1.	□	□	□	□	□
2.	□	□	□	□	□
3.	□	□	□	□	□
4.	□	□	□	□	□
5.	□	□	□	□	□

B. **¿La ciudad o el campo?** You will hear a series of statements. Each will be said twice. Circle the letter of the location you associate with each.

1. a. la ciudad   b. el campo   4. a. la ciudad   b. el campo

2. a. la ciudad   b. el campo   5. a. la ciudad   b. el campo

3. a. la ciudad   b. el campo   6. a. la ciudad   b. el campo

C. **En el campo.** Imagine that as a child you used to spend your summers in the country. Tell what you used to do, or how you used to feel, using the oral cues.

> MODELO: (*you hear*) madrugar todos los días → (*you say*) Madruguba todos los días.

1. …   2. …   3. …   4. …

D. **Gustos y preferencias.** You will hear descriptions of two people, Nicolás and Susana. Then you will hear a series of statements. Write the number of each statement next to the name of the person who might have made it.

> Nicolás: _____   Susana: _____

LOS HISPANOS HABLAN: EN TU OPINIÓN, ¿CUÁLES SON LAS SEMEJANZAS Y DIFERENCIAS MÁS GRANDES ENTRE LAS CIUDADES HISPANAS Y LAS NORTEAMERICANAS?

You will hear excerpts from several answers to this question. After you listen, stop the tape and check the appropriate boxes to describe Hispanic and U.S. cities. The following words and phrases appear in the answers.

recorrer un gran trecho	*to travel a great distance*
no hace falta	*no es necesario*
las fuentes	*fountains*
como no sea	*unless it is (unless we are talking about)*
a la par de	*al lado de*
seguro	*safe*

	LAS CIUDADES HISPANAS	LAS CIUDADES NORTEAMERICANAS
1. Son muy grandes.	☐	☐
2. Están contaminadas.	☐	☐
3. Tienen más vida.	☐	☐
4. Son menos seguras.	☐	☐
5. La gente vive *en* la ciudad misma (*proper*).	☐	☐
6. Las tiendas están en los vecindarios (*neighborhoods*).	☐	☐
7. Hay más árboles, vegetación y parques.	☐	☐

Now turn on the tape.

PRONUNCIACIÓN Y ORTOGRAFÍA:
PUNCTUATION, INTONATION, AND RHYTHM

A. Repeat the following sentences, paying particular attention to punctuation, intonation, and rhythm.

1. ¿Ya destruyeron el edificio?
2. ¡Es imposible que construyan eso en la ciudad!
3. ¿Ya hablaste con la consejera?
4. Prepararon la cena, ¿verdad? Espero que ya esté lista porque ¡tengo mucha hambre!
5. Ojalá que no perdamos el vuelo... Tenemos que estar en Los Ángeles antes de las ocho de la noche.

B. Dictado. You will hear the following sentences. Each will be said twice. Listen carefully for intonation. Repeat what you hear, then punctuate each sentence.

1. Cuál es tu profesión   Te pagan bien

2. Tú no la conoces verdad

3. Prefiere Ud. que le sirva la comida en el patio

4. Qué ejercicio más fácil

5. No sé dónde viven pero sí sé su número de teléfono

C. When you hear the corresponding number, read the following sentences. Then repeat them, imitating the speaker.

1. Enero es el primer mes del año.
2. No entiendo lo que me estás diciendo.
3. Trabajaba en una tienda donde vendían ordenadores.
4. No olvides el diccionario la próxima vez, ¿eh?
5. Nació (*She was born*) el catorce de abril de mil novecientos sesenta y uno.
6. ¿Adónde crees que vas a ir a estas horas de la noche?
7. Quiero que me ayudes a escribir esta composición.
8. Vamos a llegar al teatro temprano para que no tengamos que hacer cola.

MINIDIÁLOGOS Y GRAMÁTICA

42. **Más descripciones:** Past Participle Used As an Adjective

A. Encuesta: Hablando del cuarto donde estamos. You will hear a series of statements about the room you are in at the moment. For each statement, check the appropriate answer. No answers will be given on the tape. The answers you choose should be correct for the room you are in!

1. □ Sí   □ No   4. □ Sí   □ No

2. □ Sí   □ No   5. □ Sí   □ No

3. □ Sí   □ No   6. □ Sí   □ No

B. Descripción. Which picture is best described by the sentences you hear? You will hear each sentence twice.

1. a.

  b.

2. a.

  b.

3. a.

  b.

4. a.

  b.

5. a.

b.

6. a.

b.

C. Definiciones. You will hear a series of statements. Circle the best definition for each. ¡OJO! There may be more than one answer for some items.

1. a. el agua
   b. el aire
   c. la batería

2. a. Stephen King
   b. Descartes
   c. Danielle Steel

3. a. la mano
   b. los ojos
   c. la ventana

4. a. el papel
   b. el pie
   c. la computadora

D. Consecuencias lógicas. You will hear a series of sentences that describe actions. Respond to each sentence, telling the probable outcome of the action.

MODELO: (you hear) Escribí la composición. → (you say) Ahora la composición está escrita.

1. ... 2. ... 3. ... 4. ... 5. ...

43. ¿Qué has hecho?: Perfect Forms: Present Perfect Indicative and Present Perfect Subjunctive

A. Minidiálogo: ¿Cambio de ritmo? You will hear a dialogue followed by a series of statements. Write the letter of the person who might have made each statement next to each statement.

a = Aurelia   b = Rafael

1. ___ ¡Qué extraño que nunca hayas estado en un rascacielos!

2. ___ Siempre he vivido en una finca.

3. ___ Me estoy acostumbrando al estilo de vida del campo.

4. ___ Antes, vivía en la ciudad, pero acabo de mudarme al campo.

B. Encuesta: Hablando de lo que hemos hecho. You will hear a series of questions about what you have done. For each question, check the appropriate answer. No answers will be given on the tape. The answers you choose should be correct for you!

1. ☐ Sí ☐ No   4. ☐ Sí ☐ No   7. ☐ Sí ☐ No

2. ☐ Sí ☐ No   5. ☐ Sí ☐ No   8. ☐ Sí ☐ No

3. ☐ Sí ☐ No   6. ☐ Sí ☐ No   9. ☐ Sí ☐ No

C. Un día en la finca: ¿Qué ha pasado ya? You will hear a series of sentences. Each will be said twice. Circle the letter of the subject of the verb in each sentence.

1. a. yo   b. ella   4. a. nosotros   b. yo

2. a. él   b. nosotros   5. a. ellos   b. él

3. a. nosotros b. tú

D. ¿Qué hemos hecho hoy? Form new sentences, using the oral and written cues. Use the present perfect indicative of the verbs.

1. despertarse   4. desayunar

2. hacer las camas   5. salir para la oficina

3. vestirse

E. ¿Te puedo ayudar? You have a lot to do before a dinner party, and your friend Ernesto wants to know if he can be of help. You appreciate his offer, but you have already done the things he asks about. You will hear each of his questions twice. Answer them according to the model.

> MODELO: (*you hear*) ¿Quieres que llame a los señores Moreno? →
> (*you say*) No, gracias, ya los he llamado.

1. … 2. … 3. … 4. … 5. …

F. Un caso de contaminación ambiental. Imagine that a case of environmental pollution was discovered earlier this year in your community. Using the oral and written cues, form sentences that express what the residents have said about the incident. Follow the model.

> MODELO: (*you see*) ya estudiar el problema   (*you hear*) es probable →
> (*you say*) Es probable que ya hayan estudiado el problema.

1. todavía no avisar (*to notify*) a todos los habitantes de la ciudad

2. ya consultar con los expertos

3. encontrar la solución todavía

4. ya resolver el problema

G. Un desacuerdo. You will hear a brief conversation between two friends, Arturo and Luciano, who disagree on certain environmental issues. It will be read only once. Rewind the tape and listen again, if necessary. Complete the following sentences, based on their conversation.

1. Arturo cree que las empresas _____ _____ (ser) irresponsables.

2. Según Arturo, las empresas _____ _____ (contaminar) el medio ambiente.

3. Luciano cree que lo que _____ _____ (decir) Arturo no es totalmente cierto.

4. Luciano dice que las empresas _____ _____ (empezar) a resolver algunos de los problemas.

Now turn on the tape.

SITUACIONES

A. Y tú, ¿qué has hecho? In the following conversation, you will hear two differing points of view about the environment. Read the conversation silently as you listen.

COMENTADOR: «Desgraciadamente, el gobierno no parece tener mucho interés en cumplir con lo acordado. Esperamos que empiece a actuar antes de que sea demasiado tarde.»

ANITA: ¿Sabes? Me preocupa el problema del medio ambiente. Pero es un problema tan enorme…

JULIO: Sí, lo es, pero todos pueden contribuir con algo.

ANITA: ¿Qué has hecho tú, por ejemplo?

JULIO: Bueno, para empezar, he aprendido a bajar el termostato por la noche y a no usar tanto el aire acondicionado excepto los días de mucho calor. Utilizamos el servicio de recogida de materiales reciclables. Aún hemos empezado a reciclar el aceite para motores; hay centros que lo aceptan. Y siempre que podemos, compramos productos reciclados.

ANITA: ¿Y tú crees que todo esto ayuda a resolver los grandes problemas como la capa del ozono y la desforestación?

JULIO: ¿Ves esa taza de cartón que tienes en la mano?

ANITA: Sí. ¿Y qué?

JULIO: ¿Por qué no usas una taza de cerámica? La tienes que lavar, claro, pero te puede durar mucho tiempo. Así ayudas a salvar un bosque.

ANITA: Bueno, ¡por lo menos un árbol! No sé, Julio. Creo que ya es demasiado tarde.

B. Now you will hear a series of statements. Each will be said twice. Circle the letter of the person who might have made each statement.

1. a. Anita   b. Julio   4. a. Anita   b. Julio

2. a. Anita   b. Julio   5. a. Anita   b. Julio

3. a. Anita   b. Julio

UN POCO DE TODO (PARA ENTREGAR)

A. Descripciones. You will hear a series of descriptions. Each will be said twice. Write the letter of each description next to the drawing described. ¡OJO! There is one extra drawing. First, stop the tape and look at the drawings.

a. ___   b. ___

(Continúa.)

c. ___

d. ___

e. ___

B. *Listening Passage:* **La economía latinoamericana**

Antes de escuchar. You will hear a passage about some of the economic problems that exist both in developing nations and in more industrialized ones. The following words appear in the passage.

intentando	*trying*
digno	*worthy*
mantener	*to support, maintain*
las familias agrícolas	*farming families (families that make a living from farming)*
sin hogar	*homeless*

Listening Passage. Here is the passage. First, listen to it to get a general idea of the content. Then rewind the tape and listen again for specific information.

Después de escuchar. You will hear a series of incomplete statements. Each will be said twice. Circle the letter of the phrase that best completes each.

1. a. la agricultura
   b. la economía
   c. la emigración rural
   d. las personas sin hogar

2. a. sólo Latinoamérica
   b. sólo Sudamérica
   c. sólo los Estados Unidos
   d. los países en vías de desarrollo

3. a. hay más servicios
   b. hay menos trabajo
   c. hay un exceso de población
   d. hay muchos vendedores

4. a. la falta de educación
   b. la falta de gobierno
   c. la falta de productos agrícolas
   d. todos los anteriores

C. Entrevista: Temas diversos. You will hear a series of questions. Each will be said twice. Answer, based on your own experience. No answers will be given on the tape. Stop the tape and write the answers.

1. _____

2. _____

3. _____

4. _____

5. _____

D. Y para terminar… Una canción. "La casita" is a **ranchera,** a type of Mexican ballad or folk song.

La casita

¿Qué de dónde amigo vengo?
De una casita que tengo
más abajo del trigal,°   más… *below the wheat field*
de una casita chiquita,°   muy pequeña
para una mujer bonita
que me quiera acompañar.

Yedras° la tienen cubierta   *Ivy*
y un jazmín hay en la huerta°   *garden*
que las bardas ya cubrió,°   que… *that has already covered the fences*
en el portal° una hamaca,   *porch*
en el corral una vaca,°   *cow*
y adentro mi perro y yo.

Más adentro está la cama
muy olorosa a retama,°   muy… *smelling of broom*
limpiecita como usted;
tengo también un armario,
un espejo° y un canario   *mirror*
que en la feria me merqué.°   me… *compré*

Si usted quiere la convido°
a que visite ese nido°
que hay abajo del trigal.
Le echo la silla° a Lucero,
que nos llevará ligero°
hasta en medio del jacal.°

invito
nest

Le... *I'll saddle up*
quickly
house, hut

CAPÍTULO **15**

VOCABULARIO: PREPARACIÓN

A. Encuesta: Hablando de las relaciones sentimentales. You will hear a series of statements about personal relationships. For each statement, check the appropriate answer. No answers will be given on the tape. The answers you choose should be correct for you!

1. □ Sí □ No   6. □ Sí □ No

2. □ Sí □ No   7. □ Sí □ No

3. □ Sí □ No   8. □ Sí □ No

4. □ Sí □ No   9. □ Sí □ No

5. □ Sí □ No   10. □ Sí □ No

B. Hablando de la vivienda (*housing*)

Paso 1. You will hear Teresa's description of her housing situation. Listen carefully and check the appropriate boxes. First, listen to the statements.

1. □ Vive en las afueras.   5. □ Paga el gas y la luz aparte.

2. □ Vive en una residencia.   6. □ El alquiler incluye el gas y la luz.

3. □ Vive en una casa de apartamentos. 7. □ Tiene vista.

4. □ Vive en la planta baja.   8. □ Los vecinos hacen mucho ruido.

Now turn on the tape.

Paso 2. ¿Sí o no? You will hear a series of questions about Teresa's housing situation. Answer, according to the information in the paragraph and your completed chart. (If you prefer, stop the tape and write the answers.)

1. _____

2. _____

3. _____

4. _____

5. _____

6. _____

C. Definiciones. You will hear a series of definitions. Each will be said twice. Circle the letter of the word defined. ¡OJO! There is more than one answer for some items.

1. a. la amistad b. el corazón c. el amor

2. a. el noviazgo b. el divorcio c. una visita al consejero matrimonial

3. a. los vecinos b. los consejeros c. las casas

4. a. el noviazgo b. la boda c. la cita

5. a. la dueña b. la vista c. la novia

6. a. el alquiler b. la planta baja c. el inquilino

7. a. la planta baja b. el segundo piso c. el balcón

LOS HISPANOS HABLAN: LAS RELACIONES SOCIALES

As you might expect, social relations differ from country to country. You will hear Eduardo's impressions of the differences in social relations between the United States and his native country, Uruguay. The passage has been divided into two parts. Remember to concentrate on the vocabulary you know. Don't be distracted by unfamiliar vocabulary.

Paso 1. Before you listen to the passage, stop the tape and indicate if the following statements are true for you. There are no right or wrong answers.

1. □ Sí □ No Me gusta que mis amigos vengan a visitarme sin avisar (*without letting me know ahead of time*).

2. □ Sí □ No Por lo general, mi vida social es espontánea; es decir, generalmente, no planeo todas mis actividades.

3. □ Sí □ No Participo en actividades sociales en las cuales (*in which*) hay personas de varias generaciones (niños, jóvenes, personas de mi edad, personas mayores o viejas).

4. □ Sí □ No Para mí, la privacidad (*privacy*) es algo importante.

5. □ Sí □ No Todavía vivo con mi familia.

Now turn on the tape.

La vida social: Parte 1. The following words appear in the first part of the passage.

la falta	*lack*
extrañan	*they miss*
se dedica a	*spend a lot of time on* (*something*)
mal visto	*not looked upon favorably*

La vida social: Parte 2. The following words appear in the second part of the passage.

| la privacidad | *privacy* |
| insólito | *unusual* |

Paso 2. Now, stop the tape and write a brief paragraph that summarizes how Eduardo feels about social relations in the United States. It may help to look back at the statements you read before listening to the passage.

Eduardo piensa que... _____

_____

_____

_____

_____

_____

_____

_____

Now turn on the tape.

PRONUNCIACIÓN Y ORTOGRAFÍA:
MORE ON STRESS AND THE WRITTEN ACCENT

A. Repeat the following words, paying close attention to stress and the written accent.

1. bicicleta   centro   portero   practican   estadios

2. alquilar   feliz   tomar   legal   practicar

3. crédito   álgebra   vólibol   médico   máquina

4. corazón   natación   adiós   esquís   dirección

B. You have probably noticed that the written accent is an important factor in the spelling of some verb forms. It is also important for maintaining the original "sound" of a word to which syllables have been added.

When you hear the corresponding number, read the following pairs of words. Then repeat the correct pronunciation, imitating the speaker.

1. hablo / habló   5. gradúo / graduó   9. nación / naciones

2. pague / pagué   6. joven / jóvenes   10. francés / franceses

3. olvide / olvidé   7. diga / dígame

4. limpio / limpió   8. haga / hágalo

C. **Dictado.** You will hear the following words. Each will be said twice. Write in an accent mark, if necessary.

1. jugo   5. describes   9. sicologia

2. jugo   6. describemela   10. sicologo

3. almacen   7. levantate   11. gusto

4. almacenes   8. levanta   12. gusto

44. Influencing Others: **tú** Commands

A. Minidiálogo: La vida social de la escuela primaria: Frases útiles para la maestra. You will hear a dialogue followed by a series of statements. Circle the letter of the person who might have made each statement.

1. a. una alumna   b. la maestra

2. a. una alumna   b. la maestra

3. a. una alumna   b. la maestra

4. a. una alumna   b. la maestra

B. Encuesta: ¿Qué te decían tus padres? You will hear a series of commands that your parents may or may not have given to you when you were a child. For each command, check the appropriate answer. No answers will be given on the tape. The answers you choose should be correct for you!

Mandatos afirmativos:

1. ☐ Sí   ☐ No   3. ☐ Sí   ☐ No

2. ☐ Sí   ☐ No   4. ☐ Sí   ☐ No

Mandatos negativos:

5. ☐ Sí   ☐ No   7. ☐ Sí   ☐ No

6. ☐ Sí   ☐ No   8. ☐ Sí   ☐ No

C. Un viaje en el coche de Raúl. Form new sentences, using the oral cues.

1. (*you see*) Raúl maneja muy mal. ¿Qué le pide Ud.?   (*you hear*) no arrancar rápidamente → (*you say*) Raúl, no arranques rápidamente.

     a. ...   b. ...   c. ...

2. Cuando el coche no funciona, ¿qué le dice Ud. a Raúl? (revisar el motor) → Revisa el motor, Raúl.

     a. ...   b. ...   c. ...

D. La vida doméstica de la Cenicienta (*Cinderella*). Play the role of the stepmother and tell Cinderella what she has to do before she can go to the ball. Use affirmative informal commands for the infinitives you will hear.

     1. ...   2. ...   3. ...   4. ...   5. ...   6. ...

E. Recomendaciones. You will hear a series of situations. Respond with an informal command, based on the following verb phrases. First, listen to the phrases.

por favor, (no) decir la verdad
(no) acostarse temprano esta noche
hombre, (no) tener paciencia
(no) comer equilibradamente

(no) pelear (*to fight*) tanto con tu hermana
(no) manejar con cuidado, chico
(no) vestirse así, por favor

MODELO: (*you hear*) ¿Qué le dices a un niño que come demasiados (*too many*) dulces y que come pocas verduras o carne? →
(*you say*) Come equilibradamente.

1. ... 2. ... 3. ... 4. ... 5. ... 6. ...

F. ¡No lo hagas! You are the father or mother of the child depicted in the drawings. Tell her *not* to do the things she is doing in each drawing. Use negative informal commands. You will hear a possible answer on the tape.

MODELO: (*you see*) pegar / Isabel → (*you say*) No le pegues a Isabel.

1. saltar (*to jump*) / cama

2. poner / mesa

3. pasear / calle

4. jugar / videojuegos

5. escribir / pared

45. ¿Hay alguien que... ? ¿Hay un lugar donde... ?: Subjunctive After Nonexistent and Indefinite Antecedents

A. En la plaza central. You will hear a series of statements about the drawing. Circle **C** or **F**. First, stop the tape and look at the drawing.

1. C F   2. C F   3. C F   4. C F

B. ¿Sabe Ud. patinar? You will hear a series of sentences. Each will be said twice. Circle the appropriate letters to indicate whether the sentence refers to a known or to an as yet unknown person.

1. a. known   b. unknown   3. a. known   b. unknown

2. a. known   b. unknown   4. a. known   b. unknown

C. En busca de una nueva casa. Form new sentences, using the oral cues.

1. (*you see and hear*) ¿Qué tipo de casa buscan Uds.?   (*you hear*) estar en el campo →
   (*you say*) Buscamos una casa que esté en el campo.

   a. ...   b. ...   c. ...   d. ...

2. (*you see and hear*) ¿Y cómo quieren Uds. que sean los vecinos?   (*you hear*) jugar a las cartas →
   (*you say*) Queremos vecinos que jueguen a las cartas.

   a. ...   b. ...   c. ...   d. ...

D. Escenas de la vida. You will hear a series of statements. Each will be said twice. Respond to each statement, using the written cues.

MODELO: (*you hear*) Necesitamos un secretario que hable español.
           (*you see*) Pues, yo conozco... →
           (*you say*) Pues, yo conozco un secretario que habla español.

1. Yo te puedo recomendar...   4. Pues yo también quiero tener...

2. Lo siento, pero no hay nadie aquí...   5. Ellos van a ofrecerte un puesto...

3. Pues yo busco...

E. **¿Qué tienen estas personas? ¿Y qué desean?** Tell what these people have and what they want, using the written cues. You will hear a possible answer on the tape.

MODELO: (*you see*) viejo / nuevo →
(*you say*) Arturo tiene un auto que es viejo; desea uno que sea nuevo.

1. no tener vista / tener vista

2. perezoso / trabajador

3. grande / pequeño

4. hacer mucho ruido / ser más tranquilos

46. **Lo hago para que tú...** : Subjunctive After Conjunctions of Contingency and Purpose

A. Minidiálogo: Una tarde con la pandilla. You will hear a dialogue followed by a series of statements. Circle **C, F,** or **ND (no lo dice).**

1. C F ND   Estas personas sólo van al partido si juega su amigo David.

2. C F ND   Ya compraron los boletos.

3. C F ND   David va a jugar en el partido.

4. C F ND   También hay un partido en la televisión.

5. C F ND   Es probable que todos se queden en casa porque está empezando a llover.

B. Un viaje. You will hear the following pairs of sentences. Then you will hear a conjunction. Join each pair of sentences, using the conjunction and making any necessary changes.

> MODELO: *(you see and hear)* Hacemos el viaje. No cuesta mucho.   *(you hear)* con tal que →
> *(you say)* Hacemos el viaje con tal que no cueste mucho.

1. Tenemos que salir. Empieza a llover.

2. No queremos ir. Hace sol.

3. Pon las maletas en el coche. Podemos salir pronto.

4. Trae el mapa. Nos perdemos.

C. Descripción. Circle the letter of the picture best described by the sentences you hear. Each sentence will be said twice.

1. a.      b.

2. a.    b.

3. a.    b.

4. a.    b.

D. ¿Quién lo dijo? When you hear the number, read aloud each of the following statements, giving the present subjunctive form of the verbs in parentheses. You will hear the correct answer on the tape. Then you will hear the names of two different people. Circle the letter of the person who might have made each statement.

1. a b   No les doy los paquetes a los clientes antes de que me (*pagar*).

2. a b   Voy a revisar las llantas en caso de que (*necesitar*) aire.

3. a b   No compro esa computadora a menos que (*ser*) fácil de manejar.

4. a b   Voy a tomarle la temperatura al paciente antes de que lo (*ver*) la doctora.

SITUACIONES

A. ¿Cuándo nos vamos a ver? In the following conversations you will hear how to extend, accept, and decline invitations. Read the conversations silently as you listen.

(*Entre amigos*)

LAURA: Oye, no nos vemos nunca.

NATALIA: Sí, es verdad. Llevo una temporada en que no tengo tiempo para nada.

LAURA: Así no se debe vivir…

NATALIA: Tienes razón, pero últimamente no sé qué me pasa, que no tengo ni un minuto libre.

LAURA: Supongo que ya tienes planes para hoy, ¿verdad?

NATALIA: Pues estoy esperando que me llame Félix. Íbamos a jugar al tenis esta tarde y luego pensábamos ir al cine. ¿Por qué no vienes con nosostros?

LAURA: No puedo. Esta noche voy a cenar con mi hija y su esposo. ¿Y mañana? ¿Por qué no almorzamos juntas?

NATALIA: A ver. Mañana es jueves. Imposible. Los jueves voy al concierto de mediodía. ¿Por qué no nos encontramos por la tarde después del trabajo?

LAURA: Mañana empiezo el turno de noche y salgo muy tarde.

NATALIA: ¡Caramba! Luego me dices que soy yo quien nunca tiene tiempo, pero tú también tienes una vida muy complicada.

(*Cita para el fin de semana*)

ESTELA: ¡Por fin es viernes! ¡Qué alegría!

ALFONSO: ¿Qué vas a hacer este fin de semana?

ESTELA: El sábado Luisa y yo vamos a la playa, pero regresamos temprano. Ven con nosotros, si quieres.

ALFONSO: Gracias, pero no puedo. Hace tiempo que tengo ganas de ir a la playa, pero tengo varias cosas que hacer mañana. Tal vez otro fin de semana.

ESTELA: ¿Por qué no cenas con nosotros por lo menos? Tenemos mesa en el restaurante La Olla. ¿Sabes dónde está?

ALFONSO: Sí, y es una gran idea. ¿A qué hora?

ESTELA: Entre las siete menos cuarto y las siete. La mesa está reservada en mi nombre.

ALFONSO: Muy bien y… muchas gracias por insistir. Hasta mañana, ¿eh?

ESTELA: ¡Sí, mañana!

B. Now you will participate in a similar conversation in which you either extend or decline an invitation, as indicated by the cues. Use the cues in the order given for each conversation. You will hear the cues first.

(*Una invitación*)

1. estar libre / esta tarde

2. venir conmigo / tomar un café

ALICIA: ¡Hola Yolanda! ¡Hace tiempo que no te veo! ¿_____1?

YOLANDA: ¡Qué coincidencia! Te iba a llamar anoche. Resulta que no tengo que trabajar esta tarde.

ALICIA: ¡Magnífico! ¿Quieres _____2?

YOLANDA: Pues, ¡claro! Tengo un montón que contarte…

(*Lo siento, pero…*)

1. ¿y tú?

2. hoy no poder / ya tener planes

ARTURO: Jaime, ¿qué tal, hombre?

JAIME: Bien, bien, ¿_____¹?

ARTURO: Bastante bien, gracias. Sabes, te iba a llamar esta tarde para ver si querías ir a la playa. ¡Hace tanto calor!

JAIME: Ah… Gracias, pero _____ .

_____ 2

ARTURO: ¡Qué lástima! Quizás otro día.

JAIME: Sí. Quizás pueda otro día.

UN PODO DE TODO (PARA ENTREGAR)

A. Dictado: El viernes por la noche. You will hear a brief theater ad, followed by a brief conversation. Listen carefully, then stop the tape and write the requested information. First, listen to the list of information.

cuándo tiene lugar la función: _____

el nombre de la comedia: _____

la actriz principal: _____

el nombre del teatro: _____

el nombre de las personas que van a la función: _____, _____ y _____

Now turn on the tape.

B. *Listening Passage:* **Semejanzas y diferencias**

Antes de escuchar. You will hear a conversation, already in progress, between two students: One is from Spain and the other is from the United States. They are talking about the similarities and differences between people of their age group in the U.S. and Spain. Notice that the student from Spain uses the **vosotros** forms of verbs, pronouns, and possessive adjectives instead of the **ustedes** forms. Although the **vosotros** forms are not frequently used in *Puntos de partida,* you should be able to recognize them.

Listening Passage. The following words and phrases appear in the conversation.

independizarse	*to become independent*
me di cuenta que	*I realized*
no se ve tan mal	*it is not looked down upon (considered odd, viewed as bad)*
dura	*lasts*
el préstamo	*loan*
la beca	*scholarship, grant*
los ingresos	*earnings, assets*
estatal	*state run (adj.)*

Después de escuchar. Stop the tape and indicate the country to which the following sentences refer, based on the conversation that you just heard.

	ESPAÑA	LOS ESTADOS UNIDOS	
1.	☐	☐	La mayoría de las universidades son estatales.
2.	☐	☐	Es normal obtener un préstamo para asistir a la universidad.
3.	☐	☐	Es normal que una persona mayor de 18 años viva con sus padres.
4.	☐	☐	Se ve mal que los hijos vivan con la familia después de cumplir los dieciocho años.
5.	☐	☐	La universidad dura cinco años, generalmente.
6.	☐	☐	A los jóvenes les gusta la música rock y llevar *jeans*.

Now turn on the tape.

C. Entrevista: Temas diversos. You will hear a series of questions. Each will be said twice. Answer, based on your own experience. No answers will be given on the tape. Stop the tape and write the answers.

1. _____
2. _____
3. _____
4. _____
5. _____
6. _____
7. _____
8. _____

D. Y para terminar… Una canción. The song "**Cielito lindo**" is popular throughout Hispanic America, and it is well known in some parts of the United States.

Cielito lindo

De la Sierra Morena,
Cielito lindo,° vienen bajando,   bonito
Un par de ojitos negros,
Cielito lindo,
De contrabando.

Coro

Ay, ay, ay, ay,
Canta y no llores,
Porque cantando se alegran,
Cielito lindo,
Los corazones. (*bis*)°   *repeat*

REPASO **5**

A. *Listening Passage:* **El examen de conducir (Para entregar).**

Antes de escuchar. You will hear a conversation between a man and a woman about one aspect of driving. The following words appear in the conversation.

habíamos quedado	*we had agreed to meet*
me tocó	*I got*
antipatiquísimo	*very unpleasant*
bastante tengo con	*I have enough trouble with*
de golpe	*suddenly*
el volante	*steering wheel*

Listening Passage. Here is the passage. First, listen to it to get a general idea of the content. Then rewind the tape and listen again for specific information.

Después de escuchar. Circle the letter of the phrase that best completes each statement, based on the listening passage.

1. Estos jóvenes son…

    a. hermanos　　　　　b. novios　　　　　c. solamente amigos

2. Probablemente son…

    a. empleados de la　　b. estudiantes　　　c. profesores
       biblioteca

3. Ese día, el joven había tenido…

    a. un examen en un　　b. una cita importante　　c. un examen de
       curso　　　　　　　　　　　　　　　　　　　　　conducir

4. De la conversación, se deduce que…

    a. al joven no le gusta　　b. el joven no quiere　　c. no es la primera vez
       conducir　　　　　　　examinarse más　　　　que el joven se
       　　　　　　　　　　　　　　　　　　　　　　　examina

5. No pasó el examen porque…

    a. se saltó (*he missed*)　　b. se puso nervioso　　c. hizo mal la parte
       un *stop*　　　　　　　　　　　　　　　　　teórica

Now turn on the tape.

B. ¿Dónde están estas personas? You will hear a series of brief conversations or parts of conversations. Write the number of each next to the location in which the conversation might be taking place. First, listen to the list of locations.

___ una gasolinera   ___ un auto

___ una ciudad   ___ el campo

C. En busca de vivienda (*housing*). You will hear three housing ads. Then you will hear descriptions of people who are looking for housing. Choose the house or apartment that best suits the needs of each person. You may want to jot down notes about the ads and the people in the spaces provided.

Anuncios

Anuncio 1: _____

_____

_____

Anuncio 2: _____

_____

_____

Anuncio 3: _____

_____

_____

Personas

1. los Sres. Robles: Anuncio ___

2. Maricela y Ricardo: Anuncio ___

3. Rogelio: Anuncio ___

D. Descripción: La boda de Marisol y Gregorio. Using the written and oral cues, describe what you see in this drawing. The oral cues will give you the name of the person or persons to describe. Use the present perfect tense. You will hear a possible answer on the tape.

MODELO: (*you see*) casarse hoy   (*you hear*) Marisol y Gregorio →
                 (*you say*) Marisol y Gregorio se han casado hoy.

1. venir / a / boda
2. venir / a / boda / con / hermano
3. servir / champán

4. mandar / regalos de boda
5. ofrecer / brindis (*m.*) (*toast*)

E. *Listening Passage:* **Hablando del cine (Para entregar)**

Antes de escuchar. You will hear a brief passage about the movie industry in Hispanic countries. The following words appear in the passage.

ha crecido	*has grown*
gozan de	*enjoy*
la lengua castellana	*español*
desaparecido	*disappeared, missing*
el cinéfilo	*movie fan*
el éxito	*success*

Listening Passage. Here is the passage. First, listen to it to get a general idea of the content. Then rewind the tape and listen again for specific information.

Después de escuchar. Now you will hear a series of true/false statements about the passage. Each will be said twice. Circle **C** or **F**. You will need to infer some of the answers, based on information in the passage.

1. C F   2. C F   3. C F   4. C F   5. C F

F. Consejos (Para entregar). Your friend Estela is about to do the following things. Advise her what to do or *not* do, using informal commands based on verbs from the following list. Add any other necessary information. Stop the tape and write the answers. First, listen to the list.

(no) comer tanto/a _____

(no) llevar _____ al taller

(no) tomar _____ (curso)

(no) buscar _____

MODELO: (*you hear*) Me faltan dos cursos de idiomas para graduarme y no sé cuáles tomar. →
(*you write*) Pues, toma el francés tres y una clase de conversación.

1. _____
2. _____
3. _____
4. _____

G. Direcciones (Para entregar). Your friend Carla, who lives in another town, is visiting you. Today she plans to do some exploring of the city on her own. Using the map and words from the list, tell her how to get to the places she wants to visit. You will hear each of her questions twice. Stop the tape and write the answers. First, listen to the list.

doblar	a la derecha
seguir todo derecho	a la izquierda
la esquina	

Now look at the map. Note that your location is indicated with an arrow and a star. The destinations Carla will ask you about will be said now. You may want to circle them on the map.

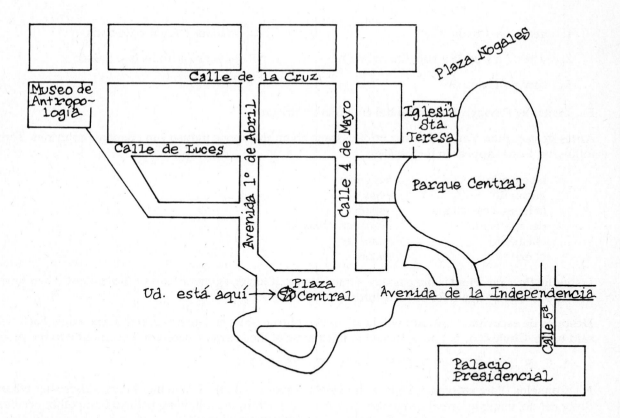

MODELO: (*you hear*) Dime, ¿cómo puedo llegar a la Iglesia de Santa Teresa? →
(*you write*) Sigue todo derecho por la Calle Cuatro de Mayo y dobla a la derecha en la segunda esquina.

1. _____

2. _____

3. _____

H. Entrevista: Temas diversos (Para entregar). You will hear a series of questions. Each will be said twice. Answer, based on your own experience. No answers will be given on the tape. Stop the tape and write the answers.

1. _____

2. _____

3. _____

4. _____

5. _____

6. _____

CAPÍTULO **16**

VOCABULARIO: PREPARACIÓN

A. Encuesta: ¿Con qué frecuencia... ? You will hear a series of statements about different ways of learning about what goes on in the world. For each statement, check the appropriate answer. No answers will be given on the tape. The answers you choose should be correct for you!

	TODOS LOS DÍAS	DE VEZ EN CUANDO	CASI NUNCA
1.	☐	☐	☐
2.	☐	☐	☐
3.	☐	☐	☐
4.	☐	☐	☐
5.	☐	☐	☐
6.	☐	☐	☐
7.	☐	☐	☐
8.	☐	☐	☐

B. El noticiero del Canal Diez. You will hear a brief "newsbreak" from a television station. Then you will hear a series of statements about the newscast. Circle **C** or **F**.

1. C F   2. C F   3. C F   4. C F

C. Definiciones. You will hear a series of statements. Each will be said twice. Place the number of the statement next to the word that is best defined by each. First, listen to the list of words.

___ una guerra   ___ la testigo

___ la prensa   ___ el reportero

___ un dictador   ___ la huelga

___ los terroristas   ___ el noticiero

D. ¿Qué creen Uds.? The following statements describe the world today. React to each, using the oral cues.

> MODELO: *(you see)* Hay tantas guerras en el mundo   *(you hear)* es lástima →
> *(you say)* Es lástima que haya tantas guerras en el mundo.

1. Las guerras *son* necesarias.
2. Siempre *va* a haber terrorismo en el mundo.
3. El petróleo va a *ser* más caro en el futuro.
4. Todavía *existen* tantas desigualdades.
5. Los ciudadanos *se quejan* mucho.
6. En muchos países no *hay* libertad de prensa.

E. Dictado: Asociaciones. You will hear several groups of words. Each group will be said twice. Write the one word in each group that is *not* related and repeat it.

1. _____   3. _____

2. _____   4. _____

LOS HISPANOS HABLAN: MÁS SOBRE LAS CIUDADES HISPANAS

When asked about some of the differences between U.S. cities and the Hispanic city in which she lives, Cecilia mentioned that some of the laws were different. As you listen to her answer, write down the effect she thinks each law or situation has on the population.

LEY O SITUACIÓN

RESULTADO

1. Un horario para volver a casa

_____

_____

2. Una edad permitida para tomar bebidas

    alcohólicas

_____

_____

3. Los chicos mayores de dieciocho años

    están en la universidad

_____

_____

PRONUNCIACIÓN Y ORTOGRAFÍA: *MORE ON STRESS AND THE WRITTEN ACCENT*

A. You have probably noticed that when a pair of words is written the same but has different meanings, one of the words is accented. This accent is called a *diacritical* accent.

Repeat the following words, paying close attention to the meaning of each.

1. mi (*my*) / mí (*me*)

2. tu (*your*) / tú (*you*)

3. el (*the*) / él (*he*)

4. si (*if*) / sí (*yes*)

5. se (*oneself*) / sé (*I know; be* [informal command])

6. de (*of, from*) / dé (*give* [formal command]; *give* [present subjunctive])

7. te (*you, yourself*) / té (*tea*)

8. solo (*alone, sole* [adjective]) / sólo (*only* [adverb])

9. que (*that, which*) / ¿qué? (*what?*)

10. este (*this*) / éste (*this one*)

B. Dictado. Listen to the following sentences. Determine by context whether or not the meaning of the italicized words requires a written accent. If so, write it in. Each sentence will be said twice.

1. Creo *que ese* regalo es para *mi*.

2. Aquí *esta tu te*. ¿*Que* más quieres?

3. *El* dijo *que te* iba a llamar a las ocho.

4. *Si, mi* amigo *se* llama Antonio.

C. Repaso: *Written Accent.* You will hear a series of words. Each will be said twice. Listen carefully and circle the letter of the word you hear.

1. a. tomas   b. Tomás

2. a. gusto   b. gustó

3. a. papa   b. papá

4. a. baile   b. bailé

5. a. interprete   b. intérprete

6. a. estudio   b. estudió

MINIDIÁLOGOS Y GRAMÁTICA

47. ¡Ojalá que pudiéramos hacerlo!: Past Subjunctive

A. Minidiálogo: Aquéllos eran otros tiempos... You will hear a brief dialogue and commentary, followed by a series of statements. Circle **C** or **F**. First stop the tape and look at the cartoon.

VIEJOS VOTANTES.—¿Recuerda cuánto tuvimos que discurrir usted y yo antes de votar hace treinta años?

1. C F   Hace treinta años, don Jorge y don Gustavo no se conocían.

2. C F   Hace treinta años, los dos nunca estaban de acuerdo en política.

3. C F   Es posible que estas personas ya no tengan las mismas opiniones.

B. Encuesta: Hablando de la escuela secundaria. You will hear a series of statements about what your life was like in high school. For each statement, check the appropriate answer. No answers will be given on the tape. The answers you choose should be correct for you!

1. □ Cierto   □ Falso   6. □ Cierto   □ Falso

2. □ Cierto   □ Falso   7. □ Cierto   □ Falso

3. □ Cierto   □ Falso   8. □ Cierto   □ Falso

4. □ Cierto   □ Falso   9. □ Cierto   □ Falso

5. □ Cierto   □ Falso

C. Recuerdos. Form new sentences, using the oral cues.

1. (*you see and hear*) Cuando Ud. estudiaba en la secundaria, ¿qué le gustaba?
   (*you hear*) estudiar idiomas → (*you say*) Me gustaba que estudiáramos idiomas.

   a. ...   b. ...   c. ...   d. ...

2. (*you see and hear*) De niña, ¿cómo era su vida?   (*you hear*) ser buena →
   (*you say*) Mis padres querían que fuera buena.

   a. ...   b. ...   c. ...   d. ...

D. ¿Qué pasó ayer en el almacén? You will hear the following statements from store employees. Using the oral cues, restate each to express a past event.

MODELO: (*you see and hear*) No *quieren* que lo hagamos.   (*you hear*) querían →
          (*you say*) No *querían* que lo hiciéramos.

1. No *creo* que tengamos que trabajar tarde hoy.

2. Pero el jefe *insiste* en que nos quedemos hasta las ocho.

3. *Es* necesario que hagamos el inventario.

4. No *hay* nadie que esté contento con estas condiciones de trabajo.

E. ¿Qué quería Ud.? You are never happy with your family's plans. What would you have rather done? Use the oral cues to tell what you preferred. Begin each sentence with **Yo quería que...**

MODELO: (*you see and hear*) Ayer cenamos en un restaurante.   (*you hear*) en casa →
          (*you say*) Yo quería que cenáramos en casa.

1. Ayer vimos una película.

2. El mes pasado fuimos a la playa.

3. Anoche miramos un programa de televisión.

4. Para mi cumpleaños, me regalaron un estéreo.

5. Esta noche mi madre sirvió patatas en la cena.

48. More About Expressing Possession: Stressed Possessives

A. Minidiálogo: En el hotel. You will hear a dialogue followed by three statements. Circle the number of the statement that best summarizes the dialogue.

1. El Dr. Méndez ha perdido su maleta y la señorita no la puede encontrar.

2. El Dr. Méndez nota que la maleta que le ha dado la señorita no es la suya y ella le da su maleta.

3. El Dr. Méndez se queda con la maleta de los señores Palma.

B. ¿A qué se refiere? You will hear a series of sentences containing stressed possessive pronouns. Circle the letter of the word to which the pronoun in each sentence might refer.

1. a. la cuenta b. las cuentas 4. a. los zapatos b. las corbatas

2. a. los papeles b. las cartas 5. a. los abrigos b. el ordenador

3. a. el asiento b. la ropa

C. Hablando de lo que nos pertenece (*belongs*). Form new sentences, using the oral cues.

(*you hear*) La *computadora* de Antonio está rota. ¿Y la tuya? → (*you say*) ¿La *mía*? Ya *la* he arreglado.

1. … 2. … 3. … 4. …

D. Preguntas: Comparaciones. Your Venezuelan friend Julio is describing his home and school environments. He wants to know how they compare to your own. You will hear Julio's statements and his question to you twice. Answer his questions according to the model, using the written cues. You will hear a possible answer on the tape.

MODELO: (*you hear*) Hay 65.000 estudiantes en mi universidad. ¿Cuál es más grande, mi universidad o la tuya?
(*you see*) Tu universidad tiene 35.000 estudiantes. →
(*you say*) La tuya es más grande que la mía.

1. Hay ocho personas en tu familia.

2. Tu coche es grande y viejo.

3. Tu apartamento es grande, bonito y cómodo. Tienes una vista magnífica y pagas un alquiler muy razonable.

4. Sólo tienes cuatro clases este semestre.

SITUACIONES

A. Hablando de las noticias. You will hear two dialogues about world events. Read the dialogues silently as you listen.

(*Hablando con una persona recién conocida que es de otro país*)

A: Ud. no es de aquí, ¿verdad?
B: No. Vinimos a este país hace unos meses.
A: ¿Por qué emigró su familia?
B: Por necesidad. La situación política de mi país era intolerable.
A: Para ser extranjero, habla muy bien el inglés.
B: Bueno, ya lo había estudiado en mi país. Y además, la necesidad es la mejor maestra.

(Hablando con una persona con quien siempre discute sobre política)

A: ¿Algo nuevo?

B: Sí. Las noticias son bastante malas. En un país la revolución está a punto de estallar. La tensión sigue creciendo en otra zona…

A: No comprendo cómo te preocupas tanto por la política cuando medio mundo se muere de hambre.

B: No es que no me preocupe el hambre. Pero son los políticos principalmente los que tienen que resolver este problema.

A: ¡Bah! La política no sirve para nada.

B: Aunque no te lo creas, la política influye en nuestra vida cotidiana. Lo que pasa es que la tuya es una actitud muy cómoda.

B. Now you will participate in a conversation, partially printed in your manual, about the latest news. Complete it, based on the cues suggested. (If you prefer, stop the tape and write the answers.)

Here are the cues for your conversation.

1. el noticiero del Canal Ocho
2. explotar otra bomba terrorista en Europa / haber muchos heridos (*wounded people*)

UD.: ¿Has oído _____?[1]

SU AMIGA: No. ¿Qué pasó? Nada malo, espero.

UD.: Pues, _____[2]

SU AMIGA: ¡Por Dios! ¿Hasta cuándo va a durar esta locura?

UN POCO DE TODO (PARA ENTREGAR)

A. Dictado: Hablando de las elecciones. You will hear a brief conversation between Alberto and Raquel. It will be read twice. Listen carefully and jot down the requested information in the spaces provided. First, listen to the list of requested information.

el nombre de la candidata que perdió las elecciones: _____

el nombre del candidato que ganó las elecciones: _____

el porcentaje (*percentage*) de los ciudadanos que votó por la candidata que perdió: _____

la cuestión principal de la campaña: _____

B. *Listening Passage:* **La vida de los exiliados**

Antes de escuchar. Stop the tape and do the following prelistening exercise.

Entre las personas de diferentes nacionalidades hispanas que viven en los Estados Unidos, los cubanos forman un grupo importante. Conteste las siguientes preguntas sobre la comunidad cubanoamericana.

1. ¿Dónde viven los cubanoamericanos, principalmente?

_____

2. Muchos cubanos llegaron a los Estados Unidos en un corto período de tiempo. ¿Por qué emigraron?

_____

3. ¿Qué tipo de gobierno existe en Cuba hoy día? ¿Cómo se llama la persona que gobierna Cuba actualmente (*right now*)?

_____

4. Los ciudadanos norteamericanos, ¿pueden viajar libremente a Cuba?

_____

Now turn on the tape.

Listening Passage. Now you will hear a passage about the immigration of a Cuban family to the United States. The following words appear in the passage.

por si fuera poco	*as if that were not bad enough*
el internado	*internship, residency*
el comercio	*business*
echar de memos	*to miss, long for*
que en paz descanse	*may she rest in peace*

Here is the passage. First, listen to it to get a general idea of the content. Then rewind the tape and listen again for specific information.

Después de escuchar. Circle the letter of the phrase that best completes each statement, based on the listening passage.

1. Esta familia, como muchas otras familias cubanas, llegó a los Estados Unidos...

   a. al principio de los años ochenta

   b. hace poco

   c. al principio de los años sesenta

2. Emigraron porque...

   a. no estaban de acuerdo con el gobierno

   b. no tenían trabajo

   c. tenían problemas con la discriminación

3. Al llegar a Florida...

   a. todo fue fácil

   b. el esposo pudo encontrar trabajo como médico

   c. fue necesario que el esposo tuviera dos trabajos en dos lugares

4. Los padres todavía...

   a. echan de menos su país

   b. quisieran vivir en la Cuba de Fidel Castro

   c. piensan que fue un error salir de Cuba

Now turn on the tape.

C. Dictado: Unas vacaciones inolvidables (*unforgettable*)

Paso 1. You will hear the following paragraph, partially printed below. Listen carefully and supply the missing words.

La última vez que _____[1] al campo para las vacaciones, todo _____[2] desastroso.

_____[3] a _____[4] dos semanas idílicas en las montañas, en una casita que

pertenece (*belongs*) a mi tío. Pero antes de que _____[5] de la ciudad, _____[6] una

llanta desinflada. Por fin _____[7] la llanta y nos _____[8] en marcha. Pero a mitad de

camino (*halfway there*) _____[9] que se nos _____[10] _____[11] el mapa y nos

_____.[12] _____[13] dos horas _____[14] por caminos rurales. Yo

_____[15] que _____[16] a la ciudad, pero mi padre _____[17] en que

_____[18] _____[19] la casita de mi tío. Bueno, la _____[20] por fin, a la una

de la mañana. Al día siguiente, _____[21] a llover y no _____[22] de

_____[23] hasta el día en que _____[24] a casa. Para las próximas vacaciones,

¡_____[25] _____[26] en casa!

Paso 2. Now you will hear a series of statements about the preceding paragraph. Each will be said twice. Circle **C** or **F**.

1. C F   2. C F   3. C F   4. C F   5. C F

D. Descripción: Escenas actuales. You will hear the following cartoon captions. Then you will hear a series of questions. Each will be said twice. Answer, based on the cartoons and your own experience. Stop the tape and write the answers.

—Lo bueno de las campañas políticas es que no te las pueden repetir.

1. _____
2. _____
3. _____
4. _____

—No veáis mucha televisión... Dentro de[a]tres crimenes y seis asaltos apagáis[b] el aparato.

[a]Dentro...*After*
[b]*you must turn off*

5. _____
6. _____
7. _____
8. _____

E. Entrevista. You will hear a series of questions. Each will be said twice. Answer, based on your own experience. Stop the tape and write the answers.

Hablando del pasado

1. _____
2. _____
3. _____

Hablando del mundo actual

4. _____
5. _____
6. _____
7. _____

F.   Y para terminar... Una canción. "Adelita" is a traditional Mexican song that originated during the Mexican revolution.

Adelita

Si Adelita se fuera con otro,
La seguiría por tierra y por mar,
Si por mar en un buque° de guerra,   *boat*
Y por tierra en un tren militar.

Y si acaso° yo muero en la guerra,   *by chance*
Y mi cuerpo en la tierra va a quedar,
Adelita, por Dios, te lo ruego
Que por mí no vayas a llorar.

CAPÍTULO **17**

VOCABULARIO: PREPARACIÓN

A. Encuesta: Hablando de dinero. You will hear a series of questions about personal finances. For each question, check the appropriate answer. No answers will be given on the tape. The answers you choose should be correct for you!

	SIEMPRE	A VECES	¡NUNCA!
1.	□	□	□
2.	□	□	□
3.	□	□	□
4.	□	□	□
5.	□	□	□
6.	□	□	□
7.	□	□	□
8.	□	□	□

B. Asuntos económicos. You will hear a series of situations. Each will be described twice. Choose the most logical response to each situation.

1. a. Dejo de comprar cosas innecesarias. b. Gasto más en diversiones.

2. a. Busco un compañero para compartir (*share*) el alquiler. b. Me mudo a un apartamento más caro.

3. a. Hablo con alguien en el departamento de créditos. b. Pago los $20,00.

4. a. Pago a plazos. b. Pago con cheque.

5. a. Pago con cheque. b. Pago a plazos.

C. Hablando de dinero. You will hear a brief conversation between two friends, Beatriz and Magali, followed by a series of statements. Circle **C** or **F.**

1. C F   2. C F   3. C F   4. C F   5. C F

D. Descripción. You will hear a series of questions. Each will be said twice. Answer, based on the drawing.

1. ...   2. ...   3. ...   4. ...   5. ...

E. Dictado: Asociaciones. You will hear several groups of words. Each group will be said twice. Write the one word in each group that is not related and repeat it.

1. _____   3. _____

2. _____   4. _____

LOS HISPANOS HABLAN:
ADEMÁS DE LOS ESTUDIOS, ¿TIENES UN TRABAJO?

Listen to the answers several Hispanic high school students gave to this question. Then stop the tape and indicate the statements that you can infer from the information given in the answers.

1.   □ Es normal que los jóvenes hispanos trabajen mientras asisten a la escuela o a la universidad.

2.   □ En vez de (*Instead of*) trabajar, muchos jóvenes participan en actividades extraescolares.

3.   □ Si un joven hispano trabaja, es posible que sea porque no asiste a la universidad o a la escuela.

4.   □ A los jóvenes hispanos no les gusta trabajar.

Now turn on the tape.

PRONUNCIACIÓN Y ORTOGRAFÍA: *COGNATE PRACTICE*

A. Repeat the following words, paying close attention to the differences in spelling between the word and its English cognate.

1. correcto
2. teoría
3. arcángel
4. químico

5. teléfono
6. anual
7. clasificar
8. afirmar

9. alianza
10. físico
11. patético
12. ateísmo

B. Dictado. You will hear the following words. Each will be said twice. Listen carefully and write the missing letters.

1. ___os___ato
2. a___ención
3. a___oníaco
4. ___eología

5. o___osición
6. ___otogra___ía
7. co___e_____ión
8. ar_____itecto

MINIDIÁLOGOS Y GRAMÁTICA

49. Talking About the Future: Future Verb Forms

A. Minidiálogo: ¡Hay que reducir los gastos! ¿Qué vamos a hacer? You will hear a dialogue followed by a series of statements from the dialogue. Tell whether each statement would add to or reduce the family's expenses.

1. a. aumentar   b. reducir
2. a. aumentar   b. reducir
3. a. aumentar   b. reducir
4. a. aumentar   b. reducir

B. Encuesta: Hablando del futuro. You will hear a series of statements about where you will be or what you will be doing ten years from now. For each statement, check the appropriate answer. No answers will be given on the tape. The answers you choose should be correct for you!

1. □ Sí   □ No
2. □ Sí   □ No
3. □ Sí   □ No
4. □ Sí   □ No
5. □ Sí   □ No

6. □ Sí   □ No
7. □ Sí   □ No
8. □ Sí   □ No
9. □ Sí   □ No
10. □ Sí   □ No

C. Dictado: ¿Pretérito o futuro? You will hear a series of sentences. Each will be said twice. Listen carefully and write the verbs you hear in the appropriate column.

PRETÉRITO   FUTURO

_____   _____

_____   _____

_____   _____

D. El viernes por la tarde. Using the oral and written cues, tell what the following people will do with their paychecks.

1. Bernardo
2. algunos empleados
3. Adela y yo
4. tú... ¿verdad?
5. yo

E. El cumpleaños de Jaime. Jaime's birthday is next week. Answer the questions about his birthday, using the written cues. Each question will be said twice.

MODELO: (*you hear*) ¿Cuántos años va a *cumplir* Jaime?   (*you see*) dieciocho →
(*you say*) Cumplirá dieciocho años.

1. sus amigos y sus parientes
2. una videocasetera
3. un pastel de chocolate
4. discos
5. feliz cumpleaños

F. Conjeturas. You will hear a series of sentences. Restate each to express probability or conjecture.

MODELO: (*you hear*) ¿Dónde vive? → (*you say*) ¿Dónde vivirá?

El nuevo empleado en la oficina: 1. ...   2. ...   3. ...

La visita de la tía Ernestina: 4. ...   5. ...   6. ...

50. Expressing Future or Pending Actions: Subjunctive and Indicative After Conjunctions of Time

A. Mafalda. You will hear the caption for the following cartoon. Then you will hear a series of statements. Circle the letter of the person who might have made each statement.

1. a. Mafalda
2. a. Mafalda
3. a. Mafalda

b. el padre de Mafalda
b. el padre de Mafalda
b. el padre de Mafalda

B. Hablando de asuntos de dinero. You will hear a series of sentences. Each will be said twice. Indicate if the sentence refers to a habitual action or to an action that is yet to happen.

1. a. Habitual   b. Yet to happen   4. a. Habitual   b. Yet to happen

2. a. Habitual   b. Yet to happen   5. a. Habitual   b. Yet to happen

3. a. Habitual   b. Yet to happen

C. Dictado. You will hear the following sentences. Each will be said twice. Write the missing words.

1. Voy a darte el dinero en cuanto _____ el cheque.

2. Nos llamarán tan pronto como _____.

3. Siempre comemos en un restaurante elegante cuando mis tíos nos _____.

4. Anoche bailamos hasta que la orquesta _____ de tocar.

D. Escenas de la vida cotidiana. You will hear the following pairs of sentences. Combine them to form one complete sentence, using the oral cues.

MODELO: (*you see and hear*) Voy a decidirlo. *Hablo* con él.   (*you hear*) después de que →
(*you say*) Voy a decidirlo después de que hable con él.

1. Elisa se va a despertar. *Oye* el despertador.

2. No voy a estar contenta. *Recibo* un aumento.

3. Voy a mudarme a un apartamento. Mis padres *venden* su casa.

4. Comeremos. *Llegan* los niños.

5. Tito, apaga la luz. *Has* terminado.

6. Quieren que les mande una tarjeta postal. Yo *salgo* del Perú.

E. Antes del viaje. You will hear a series of questions. Each will be said twice. Answer in the negative, using the written cues and the word **cuando.**

MODELO: (*you hear*) ¿Ya hiciste las reservaciones?
(*you see*) llamar al agente de viajes: No, las haré… →
(*you say*) No, las haré cuando llame al agente de viajes.

1. cobrar el cheque semanal: No, los compraré…

2. darme tu ropa: No, las haré…

3. ir al centro: No, lo conseguiré…

4. tener tiempo: No, lo llamaré…

5. ir al consulado: No, las obtendré…

F. Descripción. Tell what is happening in the following drawings by answering the questions. Each will be said twice. You will hear a possible answer on the tape.

MODELO: (*you hear*) ¿Hasta cuándo va a esperar Ricardo? →
(*you say*) Hasta que llegue Gerardo.

Gerardo   Ricardo

1. despertarla

2. recibir

3. terminar de cenar

4. llegar

SITUACIONES

A. Cambiando dinero en un banco. You will hear two dialogues about changing money in Spain. Read the dialogues silently as you listen.

(*Al entrar*)

CLIENTE: Quisiera cambiar moneda extranjera.
DEPENDIENTE: Bien. Pase a la ventanilla. Allí se la cambiarán.
CLIENTE: Gracias.

(En la ventanilla de cambio)

CLIENTE: Quisiera cambiar estos dólares en pesetas y también estos cheques de viajero.
CAJERO: Bien. ¿Ya firmó los cheques?
CLIENTE: Los firmaré ahora mismo. ¿A cuánto está el cambio?
CAJERO: Depende. El dólar en billetes grandes está a 104 pesetas, y el billete pequeño, a 102. ¿Me permite su pasaporte, por favor?
CLIENTE: Sí, aquí lo tiene.
CAJERO: En total, Ud. quiere cambiar 400 dólares, ¿verdad?
CLIENTE: Sí, eso es.
CAJERO: Firme allí abajo y pase por la Caja. Allí le darán el dinero, su pasaporte y el recibo.

B. Now you will participate in a similar conversation, partially printed in your manual, about exchanging a different amount of money. Complete the conversation, based on the cues suggested. You will hear an answer on the tape. **¡OJO!** The cues are not in sequence.

> quisiera cambiar estos cheques de viajero en pesetas
> gracias
> sí, aquí los tiene
> mil dólares / ¿a cuánto está el cambio?

CAJERA: ¿En qué puedo servirle?

UD.: _____

CAJERA: ¿Cuántos dólares desea cambiar?

UD.: _____

¿ _____ ?

CAJERA: A ciento sesenta y uno. ¿Ya firmó los cheques?

UD.: _____

CAJERA: Déme su pasaporte, por favor, y pase a la Caja con este recibo. Allí lo llamarán por este número; le devolverán su pasaporte y le darán el dinero.

UD.: _____

UN POCO DE TODO (PARA ENTREGAR)

A. Situaciones: ¿Qué cree Ud. que van a hacer estas personas? You will hear three situations. Each will be said twice. Choose the most logical solution for each and repeat it.

1. a. Teresa comprará un coche barato y económico.

   b. Comprará un coche caro y lujoso.

   c. No comprará ningún coche.

2. a. Basilio tendrá que conseguir otro puesto para pagar el nuevo alquiler.

   b. Robará un banco.

   c. Compartirá (*He will share*) su apartamento con cuatro amigos.

3. a. Luisa empezará a poner el dinero que gasta en diversiones en su cuenta de ahorros.

   b. Les dirá a sus padres que no podrá comprarles un regalo este año.

   c. Insistirá en que su jefe le dé un aumento de sueldo inmediatamente.

B. *Listening Passage:* **El Tratado** (*Treaty*) **de Libre Comercio (TLC)**

Antes de escuchar. You will hear a passage about the North American Free Trade Agreement (NAFTA). The following words and phrases appear in the passage.

se firmó	*was signed*	el acuerdo	*agreement*
vienen ocurriendo	*have been occurring*	ventajoso	*advantageous*
la empresa	*undertaking*	trasladar	*to move*
el consumidor	*consumer*	la mano de obra	*labor force*
el producto bruto	*gross national product*	la cuestión	*matter, issue*
debido a	*because of*		

Listening Passage. As you listen to the passage, take notes. Based on them, you will complete a paragraph on the passage. Stop the tape and read the paragraph to get an idea of the type of information for which you need to listen.

Apuntes (*Notes*): _____

_____

_____

_____

Después de escuchar. Now, stop the tape and complete the paragraph in your manual.

El TLC, que significa _____ de _____ _____,[1] se firmó en el año

_____.[2] Une (*It unites*) la mayor zona de comercio libre del mundo, con más de

_____[3] millones de consumidores y _____[4] billones de dólares de producto bruto

combinado. Los países firmantes del acuerdo son los tres países de _____:[5] _____,[6]

_____[7] y _____[8]

Entre los problemas que pueden resultar a consecuencia de este tratado se puede contar: _____

_____.[9]

Now turn on the tape.

C. Conversación: ¡La vida es cara! You will hear a brief conversation between Sonia and David. Then you will hear a series of questions. Answer, based on the conversation and your own experience. Stop the tape and write the answers.

1. _____

2. _____

3. _____

4. _____

5. _____

6. _____

D. Descripción: Escenas actuales. You will hear a series of questions. Each will be said twice. Answer, based on the following cartoons and your own experience. Stop the tape and write the answers. First, listen to the cartoon captions.

ᵃllantas

1. _____
2. _____
3. _____

Alí en el país de las maravillas

4. _____
5. _____
6. _____
7. _____

E. Entrevista: Hablando del futuro. You will hear a series of questions. Each will be said twice. Answer, based on your own experience. Stop the tape and write the answers.

1. _____

2. _____

3. _____

4. _____

5. _____

6. _____

F. Y para terminar… Una canción. The song "**Las mañanitas**" is a traditional song that is sung—very early in the morning—to a woman on her birthday.

Las mañanitas

Éstas son las mañanitas
Que cantaba el Rey° David   *King*
A las muchachas bonitas.
Se las cantaba así:

Despierta, mi bien,° despierta,   mi… *my dear*
Mira que ya amaneció.°   *it has dawned*
Ya los pajarillos° cantan,   *little birds*
La luna ya se metió.°   se… *disappeared*

Qué linda° está la mañana   *bonita*
En que vengo a saludarte.°   *to greet you*
Venimos todos con gusto°   con… *gladly*
Y placer a felicitarte.

Con jazmines y flores
Te venimos a cantar.
Levántate de mañana.
Mira, que ya amaneció.

CAPÍTULO **18**

VOCABULARIO: PREPARACIÓN

A. Encuesta: Hablando de profesiones y oficios. You will hear a series of statements about different types of work. Indicate your opinion about each by checking the appropriate answer. No answers will be given on the tape. The answers you choose should be correct for you!

	ME INTERESA MUCHO	ME INTERESA UN POCO	NO ME INTERESA EN ABSOLUTO
1.	☐	☐	☐
2.	☐	☐	☐
3.	☐	☐	☐
4.	☐	☐	☐
5.	☐	☐	☐
6.	☐	☐	☐
7.	☐	☐	☐
8.	☐	☐	☐

B. ¿A quién necesitan en estas situaciones? You will hear a series of situations. Each will be said twice. Circle the letter of the person or professional who would best be able to help. Do not be distracted by unfamiliar vocabulary; concentrate instead on the main idea of each situation.

1. a. un arquitecto   b. un carpintero

2. a. una dentista   b. una enfermera

3. a. una consejera matrimonial   b. un policía

4. a. una fotógrafa   b. un bibliotecario

5. a. un plomero   b. una electricista

C. ¿Quiénes son? Using the list of professions below, identify these people after you hear the corresponding number. Begin each sentence with **Es un...** or **Es una...** First, listen to the list of professions.

obrero/a   cocinero/a
peluquero/a   fotógrafo/a
periodista   plomero/a
veterinario/a   hombre o mujer de negocios

1.   2.   3.   4.   5.   6.   7.   8.

D. En busca de un puesto

Paso 1. You are looking for a new job in a large corporation. Tell how you will go about getting the job, using phrases from the following list. First, listen to the list, then stop the tape and put the remaining items in order, from 3 to 6.

___ tratar de caerle bien al entrevistador

___ aceptar el puesto y renunciar a mi puesto actual (*present*)

_2_ pedirle una solicitud de empleo

___ ir a la entrevista

___ llenar la solicitud a máquina

_1_ llamar a la directora de personal

Now turn on the tape.

Paso 2. Now tell what you will do to look for a job when you hear the numbers. Follow the model.

MODELO: (*you hear*) 1. (*you see*) llamar a la directora de personal →
            (*you say*) Llamo a la directora de personal.

E. Dictado: Quejas de la oficina. You overhear a series of statements coming from a closed-door meeting between management and employees. You will hear each statement twice. Listen carefully and write down the complaints in the appropriate blank.

Las quejas de los empleados:

1. _____

2. _____

3. _____

Las quejas de los jefes:

4. _____

5. _____

6. _____

LOS HISPANOS HABLAN: ¿CUÁLES SON LAS PROFESIONES DE MÁS PRESTIGIO (*PRESTIGE*) EN SU PAÍS? ¿QUÉ PROFESIÓN ES MENOS APRECIADA?

You will hear two answers to these questions. Then, after each answer, you will hear a series of statements about the answer. Circle **C** or **F**. The following words appear in the answers.

el agente de bolsa	*stockbroker*
la remuneración	el pago (el sueldo)
sea cual sea su profesión	no importa la profesión que tenga
la enseñanza	*teaching*
remunerado	pagado

Habla Tomás, un arquitecto español

1. C F   2. C F   3. C F

Habla Francisco, un científico español

1. C F   2. C F   3. C F

PRONUNCIACIÓN Y ORTOGRAFÍA: *MORE COGNATE PRACTICE*

A. False Cognates. Unlike true cognates, false cognates do not have the same meaning in English as they do in Spanish. Repeat the following words, some of which you have already seen and used actively, paying close attention to their pronunciation and true meaning in Spanish.

la carta (*letter*)	el éxito (*success*)	embarazada (*pregnant*)
dime (*tell me*)	sin (*without*)	el pariente (*relative*)
emocionante (*thrilling*)	el pie (*foot*)	dice (*he/she says*)
asistir (*to attend*)	actual (*current, present-day*)	la red (*net*)
el pan (*bread*)	actualmente (*nowadays*)	

B. You will hear the following paragraph from an article in a Spanish newspaper. Pay close attention to the pronunciation of the indicated cognates. Then you will practice reading the paragraph. You may want to record your reading.

El *ministro* de *Transportes* y *Comunicaciones*, Abel Caballero, ha *declarado* que el Gobierno está dando los primeros pasos para la *construcción* de un *satélite* español de *telecomunicaciones* que, de tomarse la *decisión final*, *comenzará* a ser *operativo* en 1992.

Muchos de los *componentes* del *satélite* tendrían que ser *importados*, pero al menos el treinta y seis por ciento los podría construir la *industria* española.

51. Expressing What You Would Do: Conditional Verb Forms

A. Minidiálogo: La fantasía de una maestra de primaria. You will hear a teacher's description of how she would like her life to be. Then you will hear three statements. Circle the number of the statement that best summarizes the teacher's description.

1.   2.   3.

B. Encuesta: ¿Qué harías si pudieras? You will hear a series of questions about what you might do if you had the opportunity. For each question, check the appropriate answer. No answers will be given on the tape. The answers you choose should be correct for you!

1. □ Sí   □ No   5. □ Sí   □ No

2. □ Sí   □ No   6. □ Sí   □ No

3. □ Sí   □ No   7. □ Sí   □ No

4. □ Sí   □ No   8. □ Sí   □ No

C. ¿Imperfecto o condicional? You will hear a series of sentences. Each will be said twice. Circle the letter indicating whether the verb in each is imperfect or conditional.

1. a. imperfecto   b. condicional   4. a. imperfecto   b. condicional

2. a. imperfecto   b. condicional   5. a. imperfecto   b. condicional

3. a. imperfecto   b. condicional

D. ¿Qué harían para mejorar las condiciones? Using the oral and written cues, tell what the following people would like to do to improve the world.

MODELO: (*you hear*) Betty   (*you see*) eliminar las guerras →
            (*you say*) Betty eliminaría las guerras.

1. desarrollar otros tipos de energía   4. eliminar el hambre y las desigualdades

2. construir viviendas para todos   5. protestar por el uso de las armas atómicas

3. eliminar a los terroristas   6. matar a los dictadores

E. ¡Entendiste mal! Make statements about your plans, using the written cues when you hear the corresponding numbers. Make any necessary changes or additions. When your friend Alicia misunderstands your statements, correct her. Follow the model.

> MODELO: (*you see*) llegar / trece / junio →
> (*you say*) UD.: Llegaré el trece de junio.
> (*you hear*) ALICIA: ¿No dijiste que llegarías el tres?
> (*you say*) UD.: No, te dije que llegaría el trece. Entendiste mal.

1. estar / bar / doce

2. estudiar / Juan

3. ir / vacaciones / junio

4. verte / casa

5. tomar / tres / clases

52. Hypothetical Situations: What if . . . ?: Si-Clause Sentences

A. Situaciones. You will hear three brief situations. Circle the letter of the best reaction to each.

1. a. …regresaría a casa en autobús
   b. …llamaría a la policía

2. a. …escribiría un cheque
   b. …me ofrecería a lavar los platos

3. a. …trataría de negociar con el líder del sindicato (*union*) laboral
   b. …despediría (*I would fire*) a todos los empleados

B. Consejos. Your friend Pablo has a problem with his roommates. What would you do in his place? Answer, using the oral cues.

> MODELO: (*you hear*) llamar a mis padres → (*you say*) Si yo fuera Pablo, llamaría a mis padres.

1. … 2. … 3. … 4. …

C. Las finanzas. You will hear the following sentences. Restate each, using the conditional.

> MODELO: (*you see and hear*) No le ofrecerán el puesto a menos que tenga buenas recomendaciones. →
> (*you say*) Le ofrecerían el puesto si tuviera buenas recomendaciones.

1. No le harán el préstamo a menos que esté trabajando.

2. No ahorraré más dinero a menos que controle mis gastos.

3. No pagaré las cuentas antes de que reciba el cheque semanal.

4. No te cobrarán el cheque hasta que lo firmes.

D. Dictado: Una entrevista en la dirección del Canal 45

Paso 1. You will hear the following dialogue. Listen carefully and write in the missing words.

(Continúa.)

EL JEFE: ¿Qué _____ [1] Ud. si _____ [2] un choque entre un camión y un tren?

EL ASPIRANTE: Yo _____ [3] con todos los testigos.

EL JEFE: ¿Y si _____ [4] una serie de atentados (*attacks*) terroristas?

EL ASPIRANTE: _____ [5] a ese país y me _____ [6] de todos los detalles de la situación.

EL JEFE: ¿Y si aquí _____ [7] un terremoto (*earthquake*)?

EL ASPIRANTE: Me _____ [8] debajo de mi escritorio… ¡Los terremotos me inspiran más

terror que los terroristas!

Paso 2. Now you will hear a series of statements about the preceding dialogue. Each will be said twice. Circle **C** or **F**.

1. C F   2. C F   3. C F

SITUACIONES

A. Buscando un puesto. You will hear three dialogues about jobs and careers. Read them silently as you listen.

(*Hablando de la entrevista*)

ANA: ¿Qué tal la entrevista?
MIGUEL: Muy bien. Tengo la impresión de que me llamarán muy pronto.
ANA: Me alegro mucho, de verdad. ¡Ojalá que yo pudiera decir lo mismo!
MIGUEL: ¡No me digas! ¿Qué te pasó en la tuya?
ANA: Todo iba muy bien, hasta que les dije que tengo un hijo pequeño. Inmediatamente todo cambió.
MIGUEL: Lo siento mucho, ¿eh? No debe ser así…

(*Otros amigos, otras entrevistas*)

—¿Qué tal te fue esta mañana?
—Pues no sé qué decirte. Me dijeron que me avisarían en una semana. ¿Y a ti?
—Lo mismo, pero no creo que me lo den. Tenían mucho interés en la experiencia que pudieran tener los candidatos. Como sabes, no tengo ninguna.

(*Hablando con los amigos*)

—¡Hola! ¿Ya tienes trabajo?
—¡Qué más quisiera! Me gustaría trabajar en lo mío, pero de momento no hay nada.
—Por lo visto los futuros biólogos no interesan demasiado…
—Hombre, a veces pienso que si volviera a entrar en la universidad, cambiaría de carrera. Voy a tardar en colocarme de biólogo.
—Pues, no es sólo en lo tuyo. No sé si te acuerdas, pero yo tardé medio año en colocarme. ¡Y ahora llevo siete meses trabajando!

B. Hablando con el entrevistador (Para entregar). Now you will participate in an interview in which the director of personnel is interviewing you for a job in your area, **su campo.** Listen carefully; you will hear each question only once. Answer, based on your own experience or by inventing the necessary information. No answers will be given on the tape. Stop the tape and write the answers.

1. _____

2. _____

3. _____

4. _____

5. _____

6. _____

UN POCO DE TODO (PARA ENTREGAR)

A.   Descripción: ¿Qué haría Ud.? You will hear a series of statements. Each will be said twice. Write the number of each statement next to the appropriate drawing.

a. __

b. __

c. __

d. __

e. __

f. __

B. *Listening Passage:* **El sistema universitario hispano**

Antes de escuchar. You will hear a passage about the differences between the university system in most of the Hispanic world and that of the United States. The following words appear in the passage.

la etapa	*stage*
suele durar	*usually lasts*
se matricula	*enrolls*
por lo tanto	*therefore*
una vez que	*once*
el requisito	*requirement*
la profundidad	*depth*

Listening Passage. Here is the passage. First, listen to it to get a general idea of the content. Then rewind the tape and listen again for specific information.

Después de escuchar. Stop the tape and indicate whether the following statements refer to the Hispanic world or to the U.S., according to the information in the passage.

	EL MUNDO HISPANO	LOS ESTADOS UNIDOS	
1.	☐	☐	La mayoría de las carreras duran menos de cinco años.
2.	☐	☐	Al entrar (*Upon entering*) en la universidad, un estudiante se matricula directamente en el área de su especialización.
3.	☐	☐	El estudiante tiene pocas opciones una vez que (*once*) empieza sus estudios.
4.	☐	☐	Hay requisitos «generales» como ciencias naturales, ciencias sociales o humanidades.
5.	☐	☐	El currículum es bastante estricto.
6.	☐	☐	Los estudios que se hacen para una licenciatura son bastante profundos y variados.
7.	☐	☐	Por lo general, la especialización no se «declara» el primer año de estudios universitarios.

Now turn on the tape.

C. En el periódico: Empleos. The following ads for jobs appeared in a Mexican newspaper. Choose the ad you are most interested in, based on the profession, and scan it. Then, after you hear the question, answer it based on that ad. If the information requested is not in the ad, write **No lo dice.** First, stop the tape and look at the ads. Stop the tape and write the answers.

1. _____

2. _____

3. _____

4. _____

5. _____

SOLICITA:

ANALISTA DE SISTEMAS

REQUISITOS:
- Dos años de experiencia mínima en VSE/SP o VM, DOS, JCL, VSAM, CICS, COBOL deseable
- Conocimientos de SQL, CSP

PROGRAMADOR

- Dos años de experiencia mínima en alguno de los siguientes lenguajes: COBOL (preferentemente), RPG, EDL, deseable
- Conocimientos de: DBASE III, LOTUS, DISPLAY-WRITE

Todos los candidatos deberán tener estudios profesionales (preferentemente), de 25 a 35 años de edad y excelente presentación.

Por nuestra parte ofrecemos:
- ★ Una compensación económica bastante competitiva, un paquete de prestaciones muy superiores a las de ley y amplias posibilidades de desarrollo

Interesados concertar cita al 541-30-60 y 541-61-00. Atención licenciado HERNANDEZ.

IMPORTANTE EMPRESA SOLICITA

EJECUTIVA DE VENTAS

Para Agencias de Viajes

REQUISITOS:
- Egresada de la carrera en Administración de Empresas Turísticas
- Excelente presentación
- Edad de 20 a 30 años
- Disponibilidad inmediata

OFRECEMOS:
- ★ Sueldo según aptitudes
- ★ Prestaciones de ley
- ★ Agradable ambiente de trabajo

Interesados presentarse de lunes a viernes en horas hábiles en PLATEROS 31, San José Insurgentes.

IMPORTANTE EMPRESA FARMACEUTICA, REQUIERE

QUIMICO ANALISTA

(QBP, QSB, QFI o equivalente)

REQUISITOS:
- Ambos sexos
- Edad de 25 a 45 años
- Experiencia un año en el área de microbiología
- Antecedentes de estabilidad de trabajos anteriores

OFRECEMOS:
- ★ Sueldo y prestaciones muy atractivas

Interesados presentarse o concertar cita con el Lic. FERNANDO MARTINEZ en AVENIDA 1o. DE MAYO No. 130. Naucalpan de Juárez, Edo. de México. Tel. 576-00-44.

IMPORTANTE EMPRESA TEXTIL, SOLICITA:

SECRETARIAS

Requisitos: Experiencia de 1 a 3 años, excelente presentación

AUXILIAR DE CONTABILIDAD

Requisitos: Escolaridad mínima 5o. semestre de la carrera de C.P., con o sin experiencia

Ofrecemos: Sueldo según aptitudes, prestaciones superiores a las de la ley, magnífico ambiente de trabajo
Interesados presentarse en: AV. VIA MORELOS No. 68, XALOSTOC, EDO. DE MEXICO. Tel. 569-29-00.

At'n. Departamento de Personal.

IMPORTANTE GRUPO INDUSTRIAL EN NAUCALPAN, SOLICITA:

CONTRALOR CORPORATIVO

REQUISITOS:

- Contador Público ● Mayor de 35 años ● Sexo masculino ● Experiencia 5 años en manejo de empresas Holding, Planeación Fiscal, Consolidación, Trato con Consultores y Sistemas de Información ● Casado ● Sin problemas de horario.

Interesados, enviar curriculum vitae, mencionando pretensiones, al APARTADO POSTAL 150-A, Centro Cívico, C.P. 53100, Ciudad Satélite, Estado de México. U R G E N T E .

D. Entrevista: Temas diversos. You will hear a series of questions. Each will be said twice. Answer, based on your own experience. Stop the tape and write the answers.

1. _____
2. _____
3. _____
4. _____
5. _____
6. _____ _____
7. _____
8. _____

E. Y para terminar… Una canción. "De colores" is a song from the Chicano tradition in the United States.

De colores

De colores, de colores se visten los campos°
en la primavera.   *fields*
De colores, de colores son los pajaritos que
vienen de fuera.
De colores, de colores es el arco iris° que   arco… *rainbow*
vemos lucir.°   *shining*
Y por eso los grandes amores de muchos
colores me gustan a mí. (*bis*)

Canta el gallo,° canta el gallo con el quiri,   *rooster*
quiri, quiri, quiri, quiri.
La gallina,° la gallina con el cara, cara,   *hen*
cara, cara, cara.
Los polluelos,° los polluelos con el pío,   *chicks*
pío, pío, pío, pí.
Y por eso los grandes amores de muchos
colores me gustan a mí. (*bis*)

REPASO **6**

A. *Listening Passage:* **Resumen de las noticias**

Antes de escuchar. You will hear a news brief on the radio, just as it would be if you were listening to it in a Hispanic country. After you listen to the passage, you will be asked to complete the following statements about it. Stop the tape and scan them now to get a general idea of the information to look for.

Noticia 1:

Grave maremoto en _____, de más de _____ grados en la escala Richter

Noticia 2:

Tema: _____ Mes: _____

Noticia 3:

Los _____ y los _____ se reúnen para hablar de la _____.

Lugar: _____

Noticia 4:

Visita de Carlos Salinas de Gortari, _____ de _____

Duración de la visita: _____

Noticia 5:

Propuesta del partido de oposición para _____ el precio de la _____, el

_____ y el _____, el primero en un _____ por ciento y los dos

últimos en un _____ por ciento.

El próximo noticiero de amplio reportaje será a las _____.

Now turn on the tape.

Listening Passage. The following words and phrases appear in the passage.

el mediodía	*noon*
la redacción	*editorial desk*
el maremoto	*seaquake*
sin hogar	*homeless*
el paro	*unemployment*
el portavoz	*spokesperson*
la propuesta	*proposal*
el apoyo	*support*
nos sintonicen	*you tune in to us (our broadcast)*

Después de escuchar. Now complete the statements in **Antes de escuchar.** If the information was not given in the newscast, write **No lo dice.**

B. Preguntas: ¿De quién son estas cosas? You will hear a series of questions. Answer in the negative, using the written cues to complete your answer.

> MODELO: (*you hear*) ¿El libro es de Jacinta? (*you see*) más viejo →
> (*you say*) No, no es suyo. El suyo es más viejo.

1. extranjero
2. negros
3. de lana (*wool*)

4. para balcón
5. de dos pisos y está en el campo

C. Preguntas: En busca de un puesto

Paso 1. You are an employment counselor. Interview one of your clients, using the written cues. Add any necessary words. You will hear your client's answer.

> MODELO: (*you see*) llamar / director →
> (*you say*) ¿Llamó Ud. al director? (*you hear*) Sí, lo llamé.

1. volver / empresa
2. recordar / solicitud

3. vestirse / bien
4. conseguir / puesto

Paso 2. Now play the role of the applicant and answer the counselor's questions in the affirmative or negative, as indicated. You will hear each question twice.

> 1. No,... 2. Sí,... 3. Sí,... 4. Sí,...

D. Una entrevista. Practice interviewing someone, using the written cues. Give your questions when you hear the corresponding number. You will hear a possible question on the tape, as well as an answer to your question. Use **Ud.** forms in your questions.

1. ¿dónde / ser?
2. ¿dónde / vivir ahora?
3. ¿dónde / vivir antes?
4. ¿dónde / trabajar?
5. ¿cuánto tiempo hace / trabajar allí?

6. ¿casado?
7. ¿tener hijos?
8. ¿gustar hacer / si pudiera?
9. ¿qué hacer / en el futuro?

E. Dictado: El noticiero del mediodía (*noon*) **(Para entregar).** You will hear a radio newscast. Listen carefully and write down the requested information. First, listen to the list of information.

la fecha del noticiero _____

el tiempo que hace _____

el nombre de la fábrica donde terminó la huelga _____

lo qué decidió darles a los obreros el dueño de la fábrica _____

_____

la fecha en que regresan al trabajo los obreros _____

el mes en que se jugará el campeonato _____

la temperatura alta durante los próximos tres días _____

F. Todos tenemos derechos... (Para entregar). You will hear a brief conversation between Graciela and Miguel. It will be followed by a series of questions. Answer, based on the conversation and your own experience. Stop the tape and write the answers. The following expression appears in the conversation: **lo que me da la gana** (*what I feel like*).

1. _____
2. _____
3. _____
4. _____
5. _____
6. _____

G. Entrevista (Para entregar). You will hear a series of questions. Each will be said twice. Answer, based on your own experience. Stop the tape and write the answers.

1. _____
2. _____
3. _____
4. _____
5. _____
6. _____
7. _____

CAPÍTULO 19

VOCABULARIO: PREPARACIÓN

A. Encuesta: ¿Qué hiciste en tu último viaje? You will hear a series of questions about what you did on your last trip. For each question, check the appropriate answer. No answers will be given on the tape. The answers you choose should be correct for you!

1. □ Sí   □ No   6. □ Sí   □ No

2. □ Sí   □ No   7. □ Sí   □ No

3. □ Sí   □ No   8. □ Sí   □ No

4. □ Sí   □ No   9. □ Sí   □ No

5. □ Sí   □ No   10. □ Sí   □ No

B. Definiciones. You will hear a series of definitions. Each will be said twice. Write the number of the definition next to the word or phrase that is best defined by each. First, listen to the list of words and phrases.

___ viajar a otro país   ___ una multa

___ la planilla de inmigración   ___ la frontera

___ la nacionalidad   ___ el pasaporte

C. ¿Un hotel de lujo o una pensión pequeña? You will hear a series of statements. Each will be said twice. Circle the letter of the place that is best described by each.

1. a. un hotel de lujo   b. una pensión pequeña

2. a. un hotel de lujo   b. una pensión pequeña

3. a. un hotel de lujo   b. una pensión pequeña

4. a. un hotel de lujo   b. una pensión pequeña

5. a. un hotel de lujo   b. una pensión pequeña

6. a. un hotel de lujo   b. una pensión pequeña

D. Recuerdos de un viaje al extranjero. You have recently returned from a trip abroad, and your friends want to know all the details. Tell them about some of the things you had to do, using the oral cues. Begin each sentence with **Fue necesario que... ¡OJO!** You will be using the past subjunctive in your answers.

1. ...　2. ...　3. ...　4. ...　5. ...

E. Descripción. Describe what these people are doing, using the verbs you will hear for each segment of the drawing. You will hear a possible answer on the tape. Use present progressive forms (**estar + -ndo**).

los pasajeros　los turistas　el turista　el inspector　el turista

1. ...　2. ...　3. ...　4. ...　5. ...

F. Preguntas. You will hear a series of questions. Each will be said twice. Answer, using words chosen from the following list. Make any necessary changes or additions to complete your answers. You will hear a possible answer on the tape. First, listen to the list. (If you prefer, stop the tape and write the answers.)

propina　pensión　huésped　cheques de viajero　confirmar　recepción

1. _____

2. _____

3. _____

4. _____

5. _____

6. _____

LOS HISPANOS HABLAN: UNA AVENTURA EN EL EXTRANJERO

You will hear Clara's story of a trip to the city of Fez, which is in Morocco (**Marruecos**). The story is divided into two parts. The first time you listen to the story, try to get the gist of the narration. Then listen again, or as many times as necessary, for specific information. After you hear each part of the story, stop the tape and answer the true/false items.

Parte 1. The following words and phrases appear in the first part of the story.

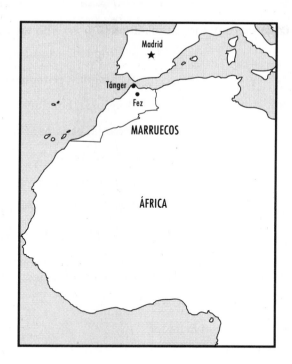

hacer transbordo	*to change planes*
Tánger	*Tangiers*
la plaza	el asiento
el croquis	*sketch*

1. C F   Clara viajó a Marruecos para estudiar árabe.

2. C F   Clara tomó un vuelo directo de Madrid a Tánger.

3. C F   El vuelo de Madrid a Tánger fue fácil.

4. C F   El aeropuerto de Tánger era muy moderno.

Now turn on the tape.

Parte 2. The following words and phrases appear in the second part of the story.

la azafata	una asistente de vuelo
el destino	*destination*
se levantasen	se levantaran
las hélices	*propellers*
chapurreado	*poor*
el sello	*official stamp*
a punto de estallar	*about to explode*

1. C F   Clara usó el color de su tarjeta de embarque para saber qué vuelo tomar.

2. C F   Todo—el avión, el aeropuerto, el pasajero que se sentó con ella—tenía aspecto de película.

3. C F   Cuando llegó a Fez, Clara ya había pasado por la aduana.

4. C F   El padre de Clara ya estaba en el aeropuerto de Fez cuando el avión de su hija aterrizó.

Now turn on the tape.

PRONUNCIACIÓN Y ORTOGRAFÍA: *NATIONALITIES*

A. Repeat the following names of countries and the nationalities of those who were born there.

1. Nicaragua, nicaragüense

   el Canadá, canadiense

   los Estados Unidos, estadounidense

   Costa Rica, costarricense

2. la Argentina, argentino/a

   el Perú, peruano/a

   Colombia, colombiano/a

   Bolivia, boliviano/a

3. el Uruguay, uruguayo/a

   el Paraguay, paraguayo/a

4. Honduras, hondureño/a

   Panamá, panameño/a

   el Brasil, brasileño/a

5. Guatemala, guatemalteco/a

   Portugal, portugués (portuguesa)

   Inglaterra, inglés (inglesa)

B. Now you will hear a series of nationalities. Each will be said twice. Repeat each and write the number of the nationality next to the country of origin. First, listen to the list of countries.

____ Chile   ____ Puerto Rico   ____ Venezuela

____ El Salvador   ____ el Ecuador   ____ Israel

MINIDIÁLOGOS Y GRAMÁTICA

53. *¿Por o para?:* A Summary of Their Uses

A. Minidiálogo: Antes de aterrizar. You will hear a dialogue followed by a series of statements. Circle **C** or **F.**

1. C F   2. C F   3. C F   4. C F

B. Reacciones. You will hear a series of statements. Each will be said twice. Circle the letter of the most appropriate response to each.

1. a. ¿Por qué no lo llevamos a la sala de urgencias, por si acaso... ?
   b. ¡Por fin!

2. a. Pero por lo menos te mandó un regalo.
   b. ¿Por ejemplo?

3. a. ¿Por ejemplo?
   b. ¡Te digo que no, por última vez!

4. a. ¿Por qué tienes tanta sed?
   b. Ah, por eso tienes tanta sed.

5. a. Por el aumento que acaban de darme.
   b. Por dos horas.

C. ¿Qué hacen estas personas? Using **por,** tell what the following people are doing when you hear the corresponding number.

MODELO: hablar / teléfono → Marcos habla por teléfono.

1. viajar / barco

2. caminar / playa

3. correr / parque

4. pagar / 15 dólares/ bolígrafos

5. nadar / mañana

D. ¿Para qué están Uds. aquí? Using the oral and written cues, tell why the people mentioned are in the locations you will hear on the tape. Each question will be said twice. First, listen to the list of reasons.

depositar dinero en la cuenta de ahorros
hacer reservaciones para un viaje a
   Acapulco
celebrar nuestro aniversario

pedir un aumento de sueldo
conseguir todos los detalles de la situación
descansar y divertirse

MODELO: *(you see)* los obreros: Están allí...
                (you hear) ¿Para qué están los obreros en la dirección de personal? →
                (you say) Están allí para pedir un aumento de sueldo.

1. Tina: Está allí...

2. el señor Guerra: Está allí...

3. mi esposo/a y yo: Estamos aquí...

4. la familia Aragón: Está allí...

5. la reportera: Está hablando...

E. La vida diaria. You will hear the following sentences followed by an oral cue. Extend each sentence, using **por** or **para,** as appropriate.

MODELO: *(you see and hear)* Hay que mandar los cheques.   *(you hear)* miércoles →
                (you say) Hay que mandar los cheques para el miércoles.

1. Salen el próximo mes.

2. Fueron al cine.

3. Estuvo en Honduras.

4. Habla muy bien el inglés.

5. A las ocho vamos a salir.

6. Venderían su coche viejo.

F. Comentarios. You will hear a series of descriptions or situations. Comment on each, using phrases chosen from the following list. Begin each answer with **Por eso...** Make any necessary changes or additions. First, listen to the list.

estudiar / ser: mecánica / maestra
caminar: parque / playa
salir mañana: Aspen / Acapulco

ir / mercado / comprar: vino /
   Coca-Cola
correr: tarde / mañana

MODELO: *(you hear)* A Alida siempre le ha gustado jugar con todo tipo de máquina. Desde que
                era muy joven sabía arreglar relojes, tostadoras y otros aparatos pequeños. →
                (you say) Por eso estudia para ser mecánica.

1. ...   2. ...   3. ...   4. ...

SITUACIONES

A. En busca de alojamiento. You will hear a dialogue in which two travelers are trying to find lodging in Madrid. Read the dialogue silently as you listen.

ALFONSO: Yo no sé cómo vamos a encontrar alojamiento. No tenemos mucho dinero, y ya es un poco tarde.

ELENA: Y el equipaje pesa mucho. No podemos ir muy lejos.

ALFONSO: Mira, en esa oficina parece que dan información sobre alojamientos. Vamos.

EMPLEADO: ¿Qué desean Uds.?

ALFONSO: Pues quisiéramos una habitación para los dos. Sólo para esta noche, pues solamente estamos haciendo escala aquí y mañana seguimos con nuestro viaje.

ELENA: Por favor, no queremos que sea muy cara. Hemos cambiado muy poca moneda. Tampoco queremos que esté muy lejos.

EMPLEADO: Bien, esperen un momento. Voy a llamar a una pensión muy agradable que no está muy lejos de la estación.

(*Pocos minutos después…*)

EMPLEADO: Sí, me dicen que hay una habitación doble, disponible todavía.

ALFONSO: ¡Qué bien! ¿Pagamos ahora?

EMPLEADO: No es necesario. Aquí tienen los datos. Este papel sirve como reserva. También les he anotado el precio. Pero, no tarden mucho en llegar…

ELENA: Muy bien. ¿Podría Ud. indicarnos cómo llegar allí?

EMPLEADO: Miren. Estamos aquí y la pensión está en esta plaza. Se lo marco en el mapa. Caminando, puede tomarles unos quince o veinte minutos. Si toman el metro, sólo son dos estaciones.

ELENA: ¡Ah! ¿Sabe si está incluido el desayuno en el precio?

EMPLEADO: Sí, lo que Uds. llaman desayuno continental.

ALFONSO: Y otra cosa. ¿Es posible dejar parte de nuestro equipaje en la estación? Mañana tenemos que volver a la estación.

EMPLEADO: Sí. Cuando salen de la oficina, a mano derecha verán la consigna. Pueden dejarlo allí.

ALFONSO: Adiós y gracias por todo.

EMPLEADO: Adiós.

B. Conversación: En la recepción. Now you will participate in a conversation, partially printed in your manual, about getting a room in a **pensión.** Complete it, based on the cues suggested. You will hear a possible answer on the tape. If you prefer, stop the tape and write the answers.

Here are the cues for your conversation.

1. media pensión
2. almuerzo y cena, por favor
3. cuatro noches

UD.: ¿Cuál es la tarifa de una habitación con _____ 1?

DUEÑA: ¿Con almuerzo y cena o con desayuno y almuerzo?

UD.: Con _____ 2

DUEÑA: Trescientos pesos la noche.

UD.: Está bien. Quisiéramos quedarnos _____ 3

DUEÑA: Muy bien. Me hace el favor de firmar aquí y de enseñarme su pasaporte.

UN POCO DE TODO (PARA ENTREGAR)

A. *Listening Passage:* **Los hispanos en los Estados Unidos**

Antes de escuchar. You will hear a passage about the influence of Hispanic culture in the United States. The following words appear in the passage.

no hace falta	no es necesario	la raza	*race (ethnic)*
descubrir	*to reveal*	teñir	*to color, tint*
pervivir	*to survive*	disfrutar de	*to enjoy*
repartido por	*spread over*		

Listening Passage. Here is the passage. First, listen to it to get a general idea of the content. Then rewind the tape and listen again for specific information.

Después de escuchar

Paso 1. You will hear a series of statements about the passage. Each will be said twice. Circle **C** or **F**. Then stop the tape and correct the false statements, according to the passage.

1. C F _____
2. C F _____
3. C F _____
4. C F _____
5. C F _____
6. C F _____

Paso 2. Now stop the tape and answer the following question.

¿Qué otros nombres, costumbres, comidas o cosas que tienen su origen en la lengua española o en la cultura hispana puede Ud. recordar? Escríbalos aquí. Por ejemplo: Hay una cosa muy bonita que se usa en los cumpleaños de los niños. Esta cosa está llena (*full*) de dulces o juguetes que caen al suelo cuando la rompen.

_____

_____

_____

_____

_____

Now turn on the tape.

B. Descripción. Circle the letter of the picture best described by the sentences you hear. Each will be said twice.

1. a.    b.

2. a.    b.

3. a.    b.

4. a.    b.

C. Hablando de las raíces (*roots*). You will hear a brief conversation. It will be read twice. After listening, stop the tape and complete the following version of the conversation you have just heard with **por** or **para,** as needed.

—Mi familia emigró _____¹ la situación política de mi país: ¡Era intolerable!

—Ah, emigraron _____² necesidad. _____³ ser extranjera, hablas muy bien el inglés.

—Tuve que aprender a hablar inglés _____⁴ sobrevivir (*to survive*) en este país. _____⁵

eso lo hablo tan bien.

Now turn on the tape.

D. En el periódico: Viajes. The following ad appeared in a Mexican newspaper. You will hear a series of statements about the ad. Circle **C** or **F**. First, stop the tape and scan the ad.

RIVIERA PAQUETES
¡OFERTA ESPECIAL!

VACACIONES...?

Venga con su familia al Hotel Riviera del Sol de Ixtapa y disfrute de un merecido descanso en las soleadas playas y tibias aguas del espléndido Pacífico Mexicano y ahorre con nuestros tradicionales:

RIVIERA PAQUETES...!!!

"RIVIERA PAQUETE DE PRIMAVERA"

3 NOCHES
4 DIAS

CON TRES DESAYUNOS

Precio por persona:
$ 80,000.00

Noche Extra:
$ 28,000.00

"PAQUETE MINI RIVIERA DE PRIMAVERA"

2 NOCHES
3 DIAS

CON DOS DESAYUNOS

Precio por persona:
$ 58,000.00

Noche Extra:
$ 28,000.00

1. C F   2. C F   3. C F   4. C F

E. Entrevista. You will hear a series of questions. Each will be said twice. Answer, based on your own experience. Stop the tape and write the answers.

1. _____
2. _____
3. _____
4. _____
5. _____

F. Y para terminar... Una canción. The song "**La llorona**" is a song of lost love.

La llorona

Todos me dicen el negro, llorona,
Negro, pero cariñoso;   (bis)
Yo soy como el chile verde, llorona,
Picante,° pero sabroso.°   (bis)   *Spicy | tasty*

Ay de mi llorona,
Llorona de ayer y hoy;   (bis)
Ayer maravilla° fui, llorona,   *marvel*
Y ahora ni sombra° soy.   (bis)   ni... *not even a shadow*

Dicen que no tengo duelo,° llorona,   *sorrow*
Porque no me ven llorar;   (bis)
Hay muertos que no hacen ruido, llorona,
Y es más grande su penar.°   (bis)   *pain*

CAPÍTULO **20**

VOCABULARIO: PREPARACIÓN

A. ¿Dónde están? You will hear a series of brief conversations or parts of conversations. Write the number of the conversation next to the location where it might have taken place. You will hear a possible answer on the tape. First, listen to the list of locations.

___ una pastelería   ___ una farmacia

___ un estanco   ___ la estación del metro

___ una papelería   ___ un café

B. Descripción. Identify the following items when you hear the corresponding number. Begin each sentence with **Es...** or **Son...**

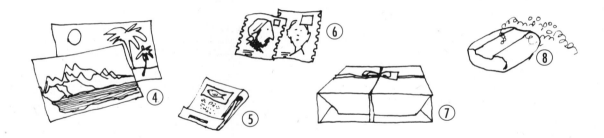

1. ...   2. ...   3. ...   4. ...   5. ...   6. ...   7. ...   8. ...

C. Conversación: En Madrid. You will hear a conversation, partially printed in your manual, about going shopping. Then you will participate in two similar conversations. Complete them, based on the cues suggested and the name of the store or place where one could buy the products named. You will hear a possible answer on the tape.

UD.: Necesito _____ .¿Quieres acompañarme?

AMIGO: Cómo no. ¿Adónde vas?

UD.: Hay _____ cerca, ¿no?

AMIGO: _____

Here is the cue for your first conversation:

       mandarles un paquete a mis padres

Here is the cue for your second conversation:

       comprar el último número de *El País*

LOS HISPANOS HABLAN: ¿QUÉ CONSEJOS LE DARÍA A UNA PERSONA EXTRANJERA QUE VIENE A VIVIR EN LOS ESTADOS UNIDOS?

You will hear Eduardo's answer to this question. As you listen, think about how his advice might apply to you if you were planning to visit or move to another country. After you listen to the passage, stop the tape and write a brief summary of Eduardo's advice. You may want to take notes as you listen. The following words and phrases appear in the answer.

la mente	*mind*
ingenuo	*naive*
extrañar	*to miss*
disfrutar de	*to enjoy*
a su alcance	*within their reach*

Apuntes (*Notes*): _____

_____

_____

_____

Resumen: _____

_____

_____

_____

_____

_____

Now turn on the tape.

PRONUNCIACIÓN Y ORTOGRAFÍA: REPASO GENERAL

A. Refranes

Paso 1. When you hear the corresponding number, read the following Hispanic proverbs, then listen to the correct pronunciation and repeat it.

1. Llamar al pan, pan y al vino, vino.

2. El agua para bañarse, el vino para beberse.

3. Quien mucho duerme, poco aprende.

4. No hay mal que por bien no venga.

5. No hay regla sin excepción.

6. No hay montaña tan alta que un asno cargado de oro no la suba.

7. Camarón que se duerme, se lo lleva la corriente.

Paso 2 (Para entregar). Now stop the tape and match the number of the Hispanic proverb with its English equivalent. ¡OJO! There is no equivalent English proverb in some cases, just a literal translation.

a. ___ He who sleeps gets swept away.

b. ___ Every rule has an exception.

c. ___ Every cloud has a silver lining.

d. ___ Every thing has a purpose.

e. ___ There is no mountain so high that a donkey loaded with gold can't climb it.

f. ___ The early bird catches the worm.

g. ___ Tell it the way it is.

Now turn on the tape.

B. Dictado. You will hear six sentences. Each will be said twice. Write what you hear.

1. _____
2. _____
3. _____
4. _____
5. _____
6. _____

UN POCO DE TODO (PARA ENTREGAR)

A. En el periódico: Anuncios. The following ads appeared in a Spanish newspaper. Look at them and choose one place in which you would like to study Spanish. Stop the tape and scan that ad. Then answer the questions you hear, based on the ad you chose. If the information requested is not given in the ad, write **No lo dice.** Stop the tape and write the answers.

(Continúa.)

UNIVERSIDAD DE CANTABRIA

CURSO INTENSIVO DE VERANO

LAREDO, SANTANDER / JULY 13-AUGUST 7

⇨ Intensive "Survival Spanish".
⇨ Cultural activities.
⇨ Sports facilities.

⇨ Housing available.
⇨ Certificate of Aptitude from
   University of Cantabria.

Fundación Ponce de León
Lagasca, 16 - 28001 Madrid
Tel. (91) 435 65 00

CURSOS DE ESPAÑQL EN
VALENCIA (ESPAÑA)
**CURSOS DURANTE
TODO EL AÑO**
4 horas diarias y alojamiento
con familias españolas
Información: C. I. L. C. E.
Bordadores, 10, 46001 Valencia
Teléfono 331 04 63

1. _____

2. _____

3. _____

4. _____

5. _____

6. _____

B. De vacaciones en el extranjero. You will hear a brief paragraph describing a series of actions and events. Number the actions listed below from one to ten in the order in which they occur in the paragraph.

First, listen to the list of actions.

___ aterrizar en Madrid		_1_ visitar la agencia de viajes	
___ hacer las maletas		___ ir al hotel	
___ recoger los boletos		___ sentarse en la sección de fumar	
___ despegar otra vez		___ bajar del avión	
_9_ pasar por la aduana		_5_ hacer una escala en Londres (*London*)	

Now turn on the tape.

C. *Listening Passage:* **Estudiando en el extranjero**

Antes de escuchar. You will hear a passage about studying abroad. The following words appear in the passage.

el idioma	la lengua
cada vez más	*more and more*
el dominio	*command (of a language)*
coherente con	*that makes sense with*
la estancia	*period of time spent in a place*
a sí mismo	*yourself*

Después de escuchar. You will hear a series of incomplete statements. Each will be said twice. Write the letter of the completion that best fits each. Not every one will be used. First, stop the tape and read the completions.

1. ___   2. ___   3. ___   4. ___

a.   ...también puede descubrir cosas importantes sobre su propia cultura.

b.   ...debe pensar en algunas cuestiones (*matters*) muy importantes, como los cursos que se ofrecen.

c.   ...pueden ser preparados por unas universidades locales o por universidades estadounidenses.

d.   ...son muy baratos para la mayoría de las personas que estudian idiomas.

e.   ...vive inmerso totalmente en el español y la cultura hispana.

Now turn on the tape.

D. Descripción: ¿Unos discos estupendos? You will hear a series of questions. Each will be said twice. Answer, based on the following cartoon. As you look at the cartoon and listen to the questions, keep in mind that the tourist in the drawing wants to go to Kiland, an imaginary country where Kiland is spoken. First, stop the tape and look at the cartoon.

(Continúa.)

1. _____
2. _____
3. _____
4. _____
5. _____
6. _____

E.   Entrevista final. You will hear a series of questions or situations followed by questions. Each will be said twice. Answer, based on your own experience. Model answers will be given on the tape for the last two questions. Stop the tape and write the answers.

1. _____
2. _____
3. _____
4. _____
5. _____
_____
_____
_____
_____
6. _____
_____
_____
_____

F.   Y para terminar... Una canción. "**Triste y sola**" is a traditional song sung by Spanish university students.

Triste y sola

Triste y sola,
Sola se queda Fonseca.
Triste y llorosa°   *tearful*
Queda la Universidad.
Y los libros,
Y los libros empeñados°   *pawned, in hock*
En el monte,°   montaña
En el monte de piedad.°   monte... *pawn shop*

No te acuerdas cuando te decía
A la pálida luz de la luna:
«Yo no puedo querer más que a una,
Y esa una, mi vida, eres tú.»

Triste y sola... (*bis*)

Minidiálogos y gramática

Grammar Section 15   A. Dictado: Minidiálogo: Cuando hay muchos invitados JORGE: Hombre, lo siento. No hay *camas* para todos, con tantas *personas* en casa. MIGUEL: No importa. Pero, dime, ¿dónde puedo dormir *esta noche?* JORGE: Bueno, *este sillón* grande es muy cómodo. Ah, también tenemos *aquella* hamaca en el *patio.* Pero yo realmente te recomiendo *ese sofá.* Es viejo, pero cómodo.

CAPÍTULO 6

Los hispanos hablan: ¿Qué te gusta mucho comer?

Paso 2. ¿Qué no te gusta nada comer? You should have checked the following boxes for each person: Clara: caracoles, oreja de cerdo. Xiomara: sopa, platos sofisticados, verduras, mondongo. Teresa: huevos, mantequilla, mondongo, hamburguesas, comida rápida.

Pronunciación y ortografía: *C, QU*

D. Dictado 1. cuatro 2. quince 3. cálculo 4. compras 5. parque 6. rico

Minidiálogos y gramática

Grammar Section 21   B. ¿Qué sabes y a quién conoces?   Paso 1. Enrique: *Sí:* bailar, mis padres; *No:* Juan, jugar al tenis, esta ciudad. Roberto: *Sí:* jugar al tenis, bailar, mis padres; *No:* Juan, esta ciudad. Susana: *Sí:* jugar al tenis, mis padres, esta ciudad; *No:* bailar, Juan.

CAPÍTULO 7

Pronunciación y ortografía: *P, T*

C. Dictado 1. Paco toca el piano para sus parientes. 2. Los tíos de Tito son de Puerto Rico. 3. ¿Por qué gastas tanto en ropa? 4. Tito trabaja para el padre de Pepe.

Minidiálogos y gramática

Grammar Section 24   A. Gustos y preferencias   Paso 1. Enrique: *Sí:* viajar, los vuelos largos; *No:* hacer cola, las demoras. Roberto: *Sí:* viajar, las demoras; *No:* los vuelos largos, hacer cola. Susana: *Sí:* viajar, las demoras; *No:* los vuelos largos, hacer cola.

Grammar Section 24   D. Dictado: Una celebración   Paso 1. 1. deciden 2. cenar 3. es 4. Julio 5. mexicano 6. porque 7. esposo 8. él 9. gusta 10. llegan 11. les 12. mesa 13. les 14. demasiado 15. orquesta 16. está 17. mejor 18. le 19. al 20. leerlo 21. le 22. quieren 23. les 24. Después 25. le 26. pastel 27. al 28. los 29. cuenta 30. pagar 31. gustaría 32. cumpleaños

CAPÍTULO 8

Los hispanos hablan: Quiero…

Paso 1. You should have checked the following items for each person: Diana: una grabadora, gafas oscuras, ropa, cosméticos, libros, una bicicleta, un radio despertador, aretes, *cassettes*, discos. José: un auto, un gran trabajo, un estéreo, ropa, una guitarra, una batería. Karen: un carro, un estéreo, ropa, un boleto de avión.

Minidiálogos y gramática

Grammar Section 26   B. ¿Qué quiere Arturo?   Paso 1. You should have checked the following for each person: su hermana: no usar su coche, prestarle su cámara; su hermano menor: bajar el volumen del estéreo; sus hermanitos: no jugar «Nintendo»

Grammar Section 26   E. Dictado: De vacaciones 1. El inspector *quiere* que los turistas *le den* los pasaportes. 2. Paquita y yo *queremos* que *vengas* con nosotros. 3. El señor Hurtado *quiere* que su esposa *juegue* al tenis. 4. Antonio *sugiere* que *vayamos* por barco. 5. La asistente *prohíbe* que *fumemos* mientras despegamos. 6. *Es necesario* que todos *lleguen* temprano al aeropuerto.

CAPÍTULO 9

Los hispanos hablan: ¿Cuál es tu pasatiempo favorito?

Paso 1. Here is the text of Xiomara and Gabriela's answers. Compare it with the notes you took.

Xiomara: Mi pasatiempo favorito es salir con mis amigas a dar paseos por la ciudad o ir a la piscina a nadar un rato. También me gusta muchísimo hacer aeróbicos en mi casa. Mi mejor amiga es Teresa y con ella es con quien salgo. Nos gusta ver los aparadores de las tiendas, ir de compras, hablar con nuestros novios, ir a buscar amigos o amigas, conversar en mi casa, tomar refrescos en las sodas, sentarnos en los bancos de los parques y ver películas.

Gabriela: Bueno, no tengo sólo un pasatiempo favorito. En realidad son muchas las cosas que me gusta hacer en mi tiempo libre. Me gusta leer y escuchar música, me gusta ir a mi club y reunirme con mis amigos. Allí practicamos deportes—tenis, natación, *squash*. Algo que hacemos muy a menudo, generalmente los fines de semana, es organizar *picnics*, y más tarde, en la noche, nos reunimos en fiestas, o vamos al cine o a algún café.

Paso 2. Answers may vary. Answers: 1. Las actividades que tienen en común las dos jóvenes son el salir o reunirse sus amigos, nadar y ver películas. 2. Algunos de los pasatiempos que no tienen en común son el ir de compras, el leer y el escuchar música.

Pronunciación y ortografía: *J, G, GU*

D. Dictado 1. Don Guillermo es viejo y generoso. 2. Por lo general, los jóvenes son inteligentes. 3. El consejero de los estudiantes extranjeros es de Jalisco. 4. Juan estudia geografía y geología. 5. A mi amiga Gloria le gustan las galletas.

CAPÍTULO 10

Pronunciación y ortografía: *Ñ, CH*

D. Dictado 1. El cumpleaños de Begoña es mañana. 2. La señorita Núñez estudia mucho. 3. Los señores Ibáñez son los dueños del Hotel España. 4. Esa muchacha es chilena. 5. Hay ocho mochilas en la clase.

Minidiálogos y gramática

Grammar Section 33   B. La fiesta de sorpresa   Paso 1. You should have checked the following actions for each person: Julia: vestirse elegantemente. Matilde: vestirse elegantemente. Tomás: sentirse mal, dormir toda la tarde, preferir quedarse en casa. Ernesto (el narrador): vestirse elegantemente.

CAPÍTULO 11

Minidiálogos y gramática

Grammar Section 35   C. En el aeropuerto: Una despedida   Paso 1. You should have checked the following actions for each person: Gustavo: estar en el aeropuerto, ir a San José, sentirse triste. la madre de Gustavo: estar en el aeropuerto, estar muy nerviosa. el padre de Gustavo: estar en el aeropuerto, estar preocupado.

Grammar Section 36   C. Dictado 1. A ellos *se les olvidó* el número de teléfono de Marta. 2. A Juan *se le perdieron* las gafas. 3. No quiero que *se nos quede* el equipaje en el aeropuerto. 4. A los niños *se les rompieron* los juguetes.

Los hispanos hablan: ¿Practicas un deporte? ¿Por qué?

Paso 1.

	DEPORTE(S)	RAZÓN POR LA CUAL SE PRACTICA
Clara	patinar	puedes practicarlo con amigos, es emocionante
Antonio	el tenis	le apasiona
Gabriela	*squash*	es entretenido y tiene mucha acción
Patricia	el tenis	es buenísimo para la salud
Teresa	caminar/nadar	son buenos para el cuerpo / no permiten que uno engorde
José	el fútbol	es saludable, divertido, emocionante
Xiomara	la natación / los aeróbicos	le gusta sentirse bien con su cuerpo y verse bonita
Erick	la natación	sirve de ejercicio físico y mental, ayuda a uno a mantenerse en forma

Paso 2. 1. la natación 2. cinco

Minidiálogos y gramática

Grammar Section 37 A. Dictado: Minidiálogo: Un resfriado muy grave ENFERMERA: ¿Cuándo *empezó* a sentirse mal? RODRIGO: Ayer por la noche *estaba* un poco congestionado. *Tosía* mucho y me *dolía* todo el cuerpo. Hoy, cuando me *desperté,* me *sentía* peor todavía. Por eso *llamé* para hacer una cita. ENFERMERA: ¿Tiene otros síntomas? RODRIGO: Creo que anoche *tenía* un poco de fiebre, pero no estoy seguro. No me *tomé* la temperatura. No *tenía* termómetro. ENFERMERA: Pues… ¡Nosotros sí tenemos! Abra la boca, por favor.

CAPÍTULO 13

Vocabulario: Preparación

F. Poniendo las cosas en orden Paso 2. Possible answers. 1. Junio es el sexto mes del año. 2. Agosto es el octavo mes del año. 3. Lunes es el primer día de la semana en el calendario hispano.

Los hispanos hablan: ¿Hay algún objeto que tenga mucha importancia en la vida diaria de tu familia?

Here is the text of the students' answers. Compare it to your notes.

Habla Diana: Creo que algo importante es el carro porque hay veces que tenemos que hacer muchas cosas y en poco tiempo. También creo que el teléfono es importante, ya que todo el día está ocupado porque nosotros llamamos a nuestros amigos y a familiares para tareas u otras cosas.

Habla Erick: Un objeto que tiene mucha importancia en la vida diaria de mi familia es el automóvil, debido a que sin él sería difícil desplazarse al trabajo o a otro lugar rápidamente y sin pérdida de tiempo.

Habla Patricia: Un objeto importante para mi familia es la mesa de cenar porque es donde nos sentamos todos a charlar.

Habla Xiomara: En mi familia, todos los objetos juegan un papel importante, pues todos son muy útiles y necesarios, pero creo que el teléfono y el auto son muy importantes en nuestro diario vivir.

Habla Gabriela: Algo que tiene mucha importancia en mi familia es el auto y el teléfono, porque nos permiten solucionar rápidamente cualquier inconveniente.

Pronunciación y ortografía: *Review of Linking*

B. Dictado 1. Todos estaban enfermos ayer. 2. A Ana le dolían los ojos y a Irma le dolía el pie izquierdo. 3. Juan acaba de ir a la sala de urgencia. 4. Carlos estaba mareado y se acostó temprano.

CAPÍTULO 14

Pronunciación y ortografía: *Punctuation, Intonation, and Rhythm*

B. Dictado 1. ¿Cuál es tu profesión? ¿Te pagan bien? 2. Tú no la conoces, ¿verdad? 3. ¿Prefiere Ud. que le sirva la comida en el patio? 4. ¡Qué ejercicio más fácil! 5. No sé dónde viven, pero sí sé su número de teléfono.

CAPÍTULO 15

Los hispanos hablan: La vida social

Paso 2. Answers may vary. Here is a transcript of Eduardo's answer. Compare it to the summary that you wrote.

Creo que una de las cosas más difíciles de aceptar al principio fue la falta de vida social. Generalmente, los latinoamericanos y los españoles dicen que extrañan el contacto social que hay en nuestros países. Aquí la gente se dedica mucho a su trabajo y usa el tiempo libre para estudiar o dedicarse a algún *hobby*. Esto, naturalmente, casi no les deja tiempo libre para los amigos. Generalmente, la vida social en los países hispanos es más espontánea. Por ejemplo, es muy común que los amigos visiten sin avisar, lo cual aquí es mal visto por mucha gente.

Pronunciación y ortografía: *More on Stress and the Written Accent*

C. Dictado 1. jugó 2. jugo 3. almacén 4. almacenes 5. describes 6. descríbemela 7. levántate 8. levanta 9. sicología 10. sicólogo 11. gusto 12. gustó

CAPÍTULO 16

Vocabulario: Preparación

E. Dictado: Asociaciones 1. el deber, la responsabilidad, los demás: *los demás*. 2. la dictadura, la prensa, el reportero: *la dictadura*. 3. el acontecimiento, la esperanza, el desastre: *la esperanza*. 4. durar, la ley, obedecer: *durar*.

Los hispanos hablan: Más sobre las ciudades hispanas

1. Hace que por la noche no haya nadie en las calles. 2. Hace que los adolescentes tomen más alcohol. 3. Por eso en las ciudades sólo hay menores de dieciocho (diez y ocho) años y mayores de veintisiete (veinte y siete).

Pronunciación y ortografía: *More on Stress and the Written Accent*

B. Dictado 1. Creo *que ese* regalo es para *mí*. 2. Aquí *está tu té*. ¿*Qué* más quieres? 3. *Él* dijo *que te* iba a llamar a las ocho. 4. *Sí, mi* amigo *se* llama Antonio.

CAPÍTULO 17

Vocabulario: Preparación

E. Dictado: Asociaciones 1. ahorrar, la tarjeta de crédito, el préstamo, prestar: *ahorrar*. 2. la cuenta corriente, la cuenta de ahorros, el banco, el alquiler: *el alquiler*. 3. el presupuesto, ahorrar, gastar, economizar: *gastar*. 4. el sueldo, el alquiler, la factura, los gastos: *el sueldo*.

Pronunciación y ortografía: *Cognate Practice*

B. Dictado 1. *fosfato* 2. *atención* 3. *amoníaco* 4. *teología* 5. *oposición* 6. *fotografía* 7. *colección* 8. *arquitecto*

Minidiálogos y gramática

Grammar Section 49   C. Dictado: ¿Pretérito o futuro? Pretérito: presté, enojó, devolví. Futuro: aprenderá, pagaremos, podré.

Grammar Section 50   C. Dictado 1. Voy a darte el dinero en cuanto *cobre* el cheque. 2. Nos llamarán tan pronto como *puedan*. 3. Siempre comemos en un restaurante elegante cuando mis tíos nos *visitan*. 4. Anoche bailamos hasta que la orquesta *dejó* de tocar.

CAPÍTULO 18

Vocabulario: Preparación

E. Dictado: Quejas de la oficina Las quejas de los empleados: 1. Siempre dicen que somos perezosos. 2. Nunca nos dan los aumentos que pedimos. 3. Creemos que ellos ganan mucho más que nosotros. Las quejas de los jefes: 4. Nunca llegan a tiempo. 5. Siempre quieren que les demos un aumento. 6. Nunca quieren quedarse a trabajar después de las cinco.

Minidiálogos y gramática

Grammar Section 52   D. Dictado: Una entrevista en la dirección del Canal 45 EL JEFE: ¿Qué *haría* Ud. si *hubiera* un choque entre un camión y un tren? EL ASPIRANTE: Yo *hablaría* con todos los testigos. EL JEFE: ¿Y si *hubiera* una serie de atentados terroristas? EL ASPIRANTE: *Iría* a ese país y me *enteraría* de todos los detalles de la situación. EL JEFE: ¿Y si aquí *hubiera* un terremoto? EL ASPIRANTE: Me *escondería* debajo de mi escritorio… ¡Los terremotos me inspiran más terror que los terroristas!

REPASO 6

A. *Listening Passage:* **Resumen de las noticias**

Noticia 1: Grave maremoto en *Nicaragua*, de más de 7 grados en la escala Richter.

Noticia 2: Tema: *sube el desempleo;* Mes: *agosto*

Noticia 3: Los *israelíes* y los *palestinos* se reúnen para hablar de la *paz.* Lugar: *el oriente medio*

Noticia 4: Visita de Carlos Salinas de Gortari, *presidente* de *México;* Duración de la visita: *tres días*

Noticia 5: Propuesta del partido de oposición para *subir* el precio de la *gasolina*, el *tabaco* y el *alcohol*, el primero en un *5* por ciento y los dos últimos en un *10* por ciento. El próximo noticiero de amplio reportaje será a las *dos de la tarde.*

CAPÍTULO 20

Los hispanos hablan: ¿Qué consejos le daría… ?

Answers may vary. Here is a transcript of Eduardo's answer. Compare it to the summary that you wrote.

Me llamo Eduardo. Nací en Uruguay y hace once años que vivo en los Estados Unidos.

El primer consejo que le daría a una persona que piensa venirse a los Estados Unidos a vivir, obviamente, sería que estudie y aprenda inglés.

El segundo, que trate de tener una mente abierta porque, lógicamente, las costumbres de aquí son diferentes. Para vivir en un nuevo país es fundamental ser abierto o, como dice un viejo refrán, «En Roma hay que hacer como los romanos». Creo que muchas personas, especialmente estudiantes que vienen por un período corto de tiempo, tienen esta idea un poco ingenua de que las cosas deben ser como son en sus países natales; de que hay costumbres «correctas» y otras que no lo son. Entonces extrañan las comidas y mil otras cosas de sus países en lugar de probar y disfrutar de todo lo nuevo que está a su alcance aquí.

El tercero, que llegue en hora a las citas sociales. En Latinoamérica, cuando invitan a una persona a una cita social y le dicen que llegue a cierta hora, todo el mundo entiende que se debe llegar más o menos tarde. Según el estereotipo, ¡sólo la gente muy aburrida llega a la hora en punto!

Por último, le diría que este país es muy grande y que hay ciudades y pueblos para todos los gustos. Con un poco de suerte, se puede encontrar un lugar perfecto para vivir.

Pronunciación y ortografía: Repaso general

B. Dictado 1. Cuando viajes a Madrid, no olvides tu cámara. 2. ¿Quisieras tomar una copita conmigo en el bar? 3. Había mucha gente en la parada del autobús. 4. Mandaría la carta si tuviera sellos y un sobre. 5. Perdón, señora, ¿dónde está la estación del metro? 6. No creo que le haya gustado el batido que le sirvieron.

About the Author

María Sabló-Yates is a native of Panama. She holds a B.A. and an M.A. from the University of Washington. She has taught at the University of Washington and at Central Michigan University, and is currently an instructor at Delta College in University Center, Michigan. She is the author of previous editions of the Laboratory Manual to accompany *Puntos de partida* and of the first through third editions of the Laboratory Manual to accompany *¿Qué tal? An Introductory Course.*